B.C.

At Your Word, Lord

How Prayer Releases the Power of God in Your Life

William L. Vaswig

AUGSBURG Publishing House • Minneapolis

AT YOUR WORD, LORD

Library of Congress Catalog Card No. 81-052272

International Standard Book No. 0-8066-1904-X

MANUFACTURED IN THE UNITED STATES OF AMERICA

To my wife Marcine, who has stood with me through life's joys and heartaches, and whose encouragement and inspiration have kept me pursuing my interest in prayer.

CONTENTS

FOREWORD

At Your Word, Lord is about the possibilities of prayer today, and is a seasoned reflection on some of the ways God's fidelity is expressed in our lives. It is also, most importantly, a story. Everyone has a story. In this book, as in its predecessor *(I Prayed, He Answered)*, are the echoes of human discoveries and disappointments that give life to what is written here. These echoes witness to the fact that this book is not a once-and-for-all decree, but an episode in a larger story of learning what it means to be a "response-able" Christian, of God's free will and sovereignty and of the puzzle of human suffering.

It is a story of honest learning, learning how to avoid grasping the future with human hands, but to listen and trust that our futures are God's future. It is a story of open dialog with God, made possible because of the oneness accomplished through Jesus the Christ. It is a story of possibilities, of hope, of daily relinquishment of self-made securities, to the end that we become servants. To be a follower of Jesus means, in part, to pray constantly.

At Your Word, Lord is concerned with the reality of this command, not as a "have-to" but as a gift, something that we long for as we long to find ourselves. We find ourselves by losing ourselves. Only within the continuous dialog of prayer, by God's initiative, is this answer to the question of who we are crystallized. This is never fully accomplished, because prayer, like the Christian life, is a sojourn. But the good news is that we can learn something about servanthood in the prayer response, that we needn't be afraid, because our ends are not in ourselves.

I can vouch for the deeply personal struggles and experienced possibilities written about here. The possibilities are not lopsided "summit" or "basin" possibilities, but are thoughtful encounters with both, encounters which at last issue in the response that Jesus is Lord in and of all things. For this story, O Lord, and especially for its teller—my father—I give thanks.

PHILIP D. VASWIG

INTRODUCTION

As a young pastor, I was deeply moved by a little book entitled *The Preacher and Prayer,* by E. M. Bounds. I was impressed with the histories of people I considered real pray-ers. I longed to be like them. Most interesting to me was the account of Martin Luther's spending two hours daily in prayer. I often wondered what he did for two hours, since I ran out of words in five minutes. I used to kneel in my office and plead that the Lord would make me an intercessor. I would ask him to lay upon my heart the needs of people, and then teach me how to pray for those needs.

He has answered that prayer. Through my parents, who brought me up to pray *about* people, I learned about the importance of intercession; through the ministry of Agnes Sanford and my own experiences, including a heart attack and open-heart surgeries, I came to learn more about praying *with* and *for* people. I learned to pray for people who came seeking help. The prayer ministry that developed out of what I learned has found a home in the Life Institute, a house of prayer in

Issaquah, Washington, where we teach and practice prayer for others.

This book grows out of my experiences of the last few years. It is intended to be a simple, down-to-earth spelling-out of the implications of prayer for our lives. I have sought to portray prayer as a response to God, and as a gift of God, which, nevertheless, is a *trainable* gift. I have used examples from our own experience and ministry of how prayer seems to work.

I would like to express my sincere thanks to my son Philip and his wife, Carrie, for their help composing, editing, and typing this book. Without them this book might not have been written. My entire family is to be thanked as well for their loving support of and involvement in the ministry.

This book is one pilgrim's way of describing one aspect of the Christian walk. Forgive any shortsightedness; many questions must go unanswered, or can only be guessed at. We still have much to learn. But I hope you find something here that inspires, comforts, or teaches. Come join me in the pilgrimage.

William L. Vaswig

1

AT YOUR WORD

In Luke 5:4-5, we hear Jesus say to Simon, "Put out into the deep and let down your nets for a catch." Simon answers, "Master, we toiled all night and took nothing! But at your word I will let down the nets" (RSV). And just as Jesus said, there was a catch, and it was good.

Perhaps you are in a position like Simon's in your prayer life. Maybe your prayers have seemed completely ineffectual for years. Maybe they drop to the floor like bubbles and burst before your eyes. Maybe they hit the ceiling, only to bounce back to the floor. You may be frustrated by God's silence. Like Simon, you have "toiled all night and [taken] nothing." But there is a faint hope within you. You may not be a daring person by nature; your family and church history may go against trying; your personal life may be in shambles; you may feel defeated by life itself. Yet something in you wants to try—for no other reason than that Christ commanded it. "But at your word I will let down the nets." For Christ's sake, you will risk. You will even risk failure. But "whoever would save his life will lose it; and whoever loses his life for my sake and the gospel's will save it" (Mark 8:35 RSV). And because Christ has commanded it, he will see to the catch.

Learning to Pray

Prayer is at the heart of the Christian faith. It is the ground of the relationship of women and men to God. Prayer was a vital part of Jesus' life; his life can't be understood apart from his reliance on and teaching of prayer. Yet so many people find that their prayer life is dry, boring, fruitless. I too have had the experience of having "toiled all night" and caught nothing. In childhood I learned the usual recited prayers: "God is great, God is good . . . ," "Now I lay me down to sleep. . . ." My family had devotions together, taking turns praying and reading. When we prayed for the sick, we prayed only *about* them, not *with* them; we always prayed to God, "Heal, *if* it be your will." We prayed for my sister's heart condition, and she died; we prayed for my mom's cancer, and she died. In seminary, we studied dogmatics, apologetics, homiletics, liturgics, Bible, and pastoral care—but never prayer. As a pastor, I prayed in church, at meetings, and in prayer groups; but each member in the groups prayed about something different, with no agreement. I had never realized the power or meaning of Jesus' words, "If two of you agree, it shall be done for you."

For years I muddled through my personal devotions, sometimes remembering to do them and sometimes not. We weren't sure that our prayers, especially those for healing, *should* be answered. Who were we to have Jesus working through us like that? "It's pride which asks with bold believing." Besides, the body wasn't quite as good as the soul; it wasn't really good enough to be saved, even though I knew the great creeds spoke of the resurrection of the body. So we talked about "redemptive" suffering, and covered ourselves by repeating what can become a "cop-out" prayer: "If it be thy will."

All that changed when I met with a situation where I desperately needed my prayers to be answered. That story is told in my book *I Prayed, He Answered.* When our son was diagnosed as paranoid schizophrenic, in our desperation we turned finally to Agnes Sanford, the gifted author of the little classic *The Healing Light.* God used her prayers to bring about the complete healing of our son. Our concept of prayer had to be completely changed. Through Agnes, I learned how to put new life into my prayers, and in subsequent years I have learned more about prayer than I ever imagined. I have learned about the prayer of faith: asking, and believing that you will receive it. And I have learned to listen to God in contemplative prayer.

I learned that I can, and should, do what Jesus did. "In truth, in very truth I tell you, he who has faith in me will do what I am doing; and he will do greater things still because I am going to the Father" (John 14:12). I always thought the "greater things" were fulfilled at Pentecost (after all, Jesus never saw 3000 converted at once, as his disciples did), and that even to think that Jesus could be referring to anyone but his immediate disciples was almost blasphemy. My attitude was always, "Shut that door"—don't expect God to do anything through your prayers. I thought that God never breaks into this closed system of a universe, and wouldn't change anything in the natural order of things. But the church has always taught the basic goodness of the body and the physical world as a creation of God, though now in a fallen state along with the mind and spirit. Illness and death are intruders, like war, but God's intention for us is wholeness.

Why did God make our bodies with immune systems if he didn't want us well? Why did he give us the will to live, and that fantastic ability of the body to heal itself? And indeed, why do we go to doctors if there isn't something in us that wants to be well? I began to see prayer and healing in the light of the first article of the Creed, as part of creation, and not only as a miraculous intervention.

And we found out that just as God hears our prayers, we can listen to him, and that contemplative prayer, far from being an esoteric practice for monks and nuns or adherents of eastern religions and Transcendental Meditation, can be used daily as a way of communicating with God. Learning these things changed my prayer life and that of my family; I now know the experience of "getting through" in prayer, of being used as a vehicle to bless and heal the suffering. A transformed prayer life is within everyone's asking.

I have come to understand prayer mainly as a response to God, although that response is God-induced. We do not seek God, on our own terms, through prayer; Christianity is not a search for enlightenment. Rather, God touches us, and we respond. We pray because it is our nature to respond to God. We are *response-able*. That may be the essence of the "image of God" in us. The more we know God, the more responsible we become. We pray because we are commanded to pray: "And whatever you pray for in faith you will receive" (Matt. 21:22). "Is anyone among you in trouble? He should turn to prayer" (James 5:13). "Be always joyful; pray continually; give thanks whatever happens; for this is what God in Christ wills for you" (1 Thess. 5:16-18). "The Lord is near; have no anxiety, but in everything make your requests known to God in prayer and petition with thanksgiving" (Phil. 4:6). We pray because Jesus prayed. He prayed for the sick; he purposively went out early to "lonely places" where he prayed; he prayed before miracles, before he chose disciples, in the garden, on the cross. I suspect that he spent a great deal of time in prayer. His praying was so obvious and appealing that the disciples sought to emulate him. They didn't say, "Lord, teach us to teach, preach, and work miracles." They asked him, "Lord, teach us to pray." It appears as if prayer is the only activity he taught them directly.

Types of Prayer

There are a number of different kinds of prayer. I would divide them into two main types: *spoken* prayer and *contemplative* prayer. I divide prayer into these two types because they point out the dialogical nature of prayer, an exchange of speaking and listening. Of the first type, spoken prayer, or talking to God, whether aloud or silently, there are probably two kinds: prayers of *worship*—such as prayers of praise, thanksgiving, and adoration—and prayers of *petition* or intercession, in which we bring our needs and wishes to God. The prayer of worship would include any expression of thanks to God or utterance of praise. Much of the prayer in our worship services is prayer of praise and thanksgiving, but these prayers are often neglected in personal devotions. Prayers of petition would include prayers for healing, prayers for wisdom and guidance, prayers for the repair of relationships. When most of us think of prayer, we think of the prayer of petition. There are other kinds of prayer, such as prayers of complaint, imprecatory prayers, affirmation prayers and so on, but most spoken prayers fall under the two categories of worship and petition.

Contemplative prayer can be described as *listening* prayer, as opposed to prayer in which you are talking to God. Unfortunately, most of us in our lives (including our prayer life) do too much talking and not enough listening. Christian meditation is a kind of listening prayer. In meditation we just sit quietly before God. It is to "Be still, and know that I am God" (Psalm 46:10 RSV). It is just waiting on the Lord to do what he wants. It is opening yourself up to God, letting him know you (though he already does), and bringing yourself to know him. In meditation I may fix my attention on a single word, such as "Jesus" or "Father"; I may use a Bible story, imagining myself in the midst of the events described in it; or I may imagine myself meeting Jesus somewhere and talking with him. In any case, in meditation you become aware of the presence of God, and then listen for whatever he may have for you.

Each of these kinds of prayer should have a place in the Christian life. Each one has a purpose and a special meaning and use. Each kind can be used in private, in a group of two or more, and in large groups. We can pray by ourselves, and we can pray with and for others. To limit yourself to one kind of prayer—speaking without listening or listening without speaking—is to cheat yourself of many rich experiences and to ignore the dialogical nature of prayer. You can find a new world in trying unfamiliar kinds of prayer, even kinds that seem risky to you. "Put out into the deep," said Jesus to Peter. Even if you are already familiar with the different kinds of prayer and use them regularly, you may feel vaguely dissatisfied with your prayer life; perhaps your prayers seem dry and too routine. In that case, you can learn how to pray the prayer of faith, "knowing it shall be so," and you can learn how to use the imagination God has given you to vary and expand your prayer life. I can give you a few hints on how you might do this.

Expanding Your Prayer Life

A good place to begin examining and improving your prayer life is with your daily devotions. Everyone needs a "quiet time," preferably at least once daily, in which to pray, read Bible passages, and meditate. Morning is probably the best time for most people; you may find it well worth your while to rise 15 minutes earlier in order to make time for devotions before the bustle of the day begins. I like to take my first cup of coffee with me into a private room or out to the patio, if the weather is suitable. Noontime and the evening can also be acceptable times for devotions, if your schedule indicates it. It is best to choose the same place every day to have your devotions, if at all possible. If you can keep the arrangements the same, you will be free to devote your energies to your prayers.

Experiment to find the time and place that work best for you. Find a time when you will not be too sleepy, when your home is quiet, and find a place that is comfortable and private. You may find that looking at a pleasant view out the window helps you to concentrate. You will also have to experiment to find a position that is most conducive to prayer. Lying down is not the best way, since your body associates this position with going to sleep and will probably oblige by doing so. Any position which is not so uncomfortable as to be distracting, but which puts you into a reverent mood, will probably be good. You may want to vary your position according to your mood of worship, kneeling one day and sitting the next. You may even want to lie prostrate, face down on the floor, a time-honored position that your body won't associate with sleep, but which will induce a feeling of reverence before God.

It is a good idea to vary the form and content of your devotions from day to day, to suit your needs and to keep your interest alive. I usually sit and look out the window and focus on God the Father, Jesus, and the Holy Spirit. It is important then to begin by protecting yourself from any evil or misleading thoughts that may come to you during the vulnerable time of prayer. Agnes Sanford taught me to use the imagery of Eph. 6:13-17 for protection. I make the sign of the cross over my body as a recollection of the sign made over me at my baptism, and as a symbol of rededication to that cross and as an external remembrance of deeply hallowed needs and gifts; I cover myself in my imagination with the cleansing blood of Jesus Christ; and I circle myself, again in my imagination, with the light of God's presence. I do this same "shielding" for each member of my family. I may say out loud or quietly, "I seal myself with the sign of the cross. I cover myself with the blood of Jesus Christ. I circle myself with the light of God's presence, so that nothing can come through to harm me."

When you have protected yourself, you can begin your devotions. You may wish to begin by "putting" yourself in the presence of God. You need to "center down," to quiet your mind and assure yourself that you are in the presence of God. You may wish to praise God, to pray the Lord's Prayer, recite one of the creeds, or repeat a Bible verse or familiar chapter. You may just wish to look out the window at a beautiful scene. Perhaps there is a picture you like to look at. My wife, Marcine, has a picture of a lamb being held by Jesus which she contemplates before prayer. You may just repeat the names, "Jesus," "Abba," "Father," and so on. You may repeat the famous Jesus Prayer, "Lord Jesus Christ, Son of God, have mercy upon me," or Agnes Sanford's version, "Lord Jesus Christ, Son of God, fill me with your light and your love." When you feel satisfied that you are "centered down" for prayer, you might wish to confess your sins and ask God's forgiveness. Then you may bring before God your petitions, requests, complaints, feelings, thanks. Just talk to God as you would to a loving father, for that is what he is.

Then you might want to meditate, using a meditation someone else has written, or starting with a Bible story and putting yourself in the situation; or you may want to imagine yourself meeting Jesus somewhere and talking to him. Meditation is the time to use your imagination, or rather to let God use it. It is also the time to listen, to hear with your heart. Ask God what he has to say to you today, and then listen for the answer. I often keep my journal by me and write down what comes to me at this time. The important thing is to allow sufficient time to listen to God and hear what he has to say, whether it is a sentence or a word or a Bible verse or a picture. You could close your devotions with a word of thanks and praise for God, and with the word *Amen*—"Let it be so."

You should not feel bound to follow any routine. Be flexible enough to let the Spirit lead you. Some days you may wish to spend the entire devotion time in meditation, some days with petitions, some days in praise. You may wish to have a meditation time apart from your prayer time. Your devotions are not the time for a Bible study; that should be in addition to your prayers. Keep the Bible reading down to short portions into which you can delve deeply. Savor the reading. Do not be afraid to be honest with God. This is the time to open up your whole self to him.

Overcoming Hindrances

You are bound to run into frustration and problems in prayer; it helps to know what you are up against and how you may be able to overcome it. I suppose the two chief hindrances to prayer are enslavement to feeling and wandering thoughts. Some people believe that they are not being honest if they pray when they don't feel like it. The opposite comes nearer the truth. When we pray because we feel like it, we are pleasing ourselves. We want to pray, and we do pray, and our prayer is acceptable to God to the degree that our will is in harmony with his. But when we pray not feeling like it, we bring God not only the content of our prayers, but also a disciplined spirit. We have kept our appointment with him against disinclination. We have displeased ourselves in order to please God. Feelings can be good, and never to know the ecstasy of religion would be sad, but feelings are too variable to be the guide in our praying. Even if you have to drag yourself into prayer, you will be welcome. God remembers that we are dust. You may find that once you take the step of putting yourself into a prayerful attitude, particularly if you kneel for prayer, your body will send a message to your heart and quicken your desire to pray.

By the same token, you ought not to judge your prayers by

the feelings you get from them. We cannot always be on the heights. Some days you may not feel that you have gotten anything out of your prayers: you may confess and yet not feel forgiven; you may try to meditate and yet not really feel restful in spirit. I am reminded of my old seminary professor, Iver Iverson, who said to me once in his Norwegian accent, "The trouble with you, Vaswig, is that you think that every time you read the Word you have to get a kick out of it." Our feelings may vary with our health, the weather, or what we have eaten lately. Just because you don't always feel loving toward your husband or wife doesn't mean you should divorce him or her. We must remain faithful through the lean times as well as the fat.

The second chief hindrance to prayer, wandering thoughts, is one that has plagued me. I'm sure that the most devout person will never find complete deliverance from this hindrance. One's power to remain in concentration in prayer will grow, and skill will finally come in outwitting the tendency of the mind to roam. Attention is the key word in prayer and meditation, just as it is in any conversation with a human being. But the permanent emancipation from this difficulty can probably never be expected.

I have learned over the years in my own battle with wandering thoughts to turn the wanderings into prayers. Instead of fighting the thoughts, I lift them into prayers. If my thoughts concern the duties that are going to face me that day, I lift them up before God in prayer before I ever come to them. It also helps if you offer the prayer vocally, in a breath or murmur, no matter how quietly, as long as it is still out loud. The lips and ears come to the aid of the mind and beat back distracting thoughts. If all else fails, recite a prayer, from memory or reading from a book. I have also learned that sometimes I just have to apologize to the Lord and give him back my undivided attention.

Praying the Psalms

I have found that the Psalms have enormous devotional value. They are used in worship settings in most Roman Catholic and Protestant churches. They can also be used with great benefit in private prayers. The Psalms are the prayer book of the Bible. The Psalms are written as poetry, and cover the whole spectrum of human concerns in prayer. The Psalms include requests and even demands. We can learn from the psalmist a respectful intimacy with God. The psalmist, in his complaints and requests, is affirming his neediness before God. A great number of psalms are prayers of praise. The psalms designated by biblical scholars as "hymns" are particularly significant in that their purpose is simply to celebrate the glories of God. These hymn psalms open with an invitation to praise God, and then, in the body of the psalm, various motives are given for praise of such things as God's saving work for his people or the wonder of God's work of creation.

I find that no other part of the Bible articulates my feelings as well as the Psalms. "Out of the depths I cry to thee, O Lord!" (RSV) are the first words of Psalm 130, which I speak out loud from memory in times of distress or when I feel myself in the depths of sorrow or despair. When you feel at a loss for words, either because of the depth of your sorrow or because of the height of your awe and joy, the Psalms may be able to express your feelings for you. Jesus' deepest feelings of being rejected by his own Father were expressed on the cross in the words of Psalm 22, "My God, my God, why hast thou forsaken me?" (RSV).

Once you have begun to find comfort and satisfaction in your daily prayers, you will find that you want to learn and experience more and more. You will want to know how to pray about certain things; you will find that you are called upon to pray for others; you will find your heart yearning to know God better and better. You will find particularly that many questions come to mind. You are embarking on an adventure in prayer. God has called you, through his Son, by the power of his Holy Spirit. At his word, you have responded. Let's begin our adventures in prayer by talking about the subject and object, end and means of our prayers, God.

2

GOD AND PRAYER

A difficulty many people have in beginning and developing their prayer life is in knowing how to address God. Do we address God as a friend, a father, a king, an abstract source of energy, or the "ground of all being"? Do we pray persuasively, in order to convince God or change his mind, or should we pray passively, not venturing to ask anything? Do we talk with God about everything, or should we keep the bad things from him? These are important questions, ones which are bound to come to you once you stop taking prayer for granted and start taking it seriously.

These sorts of questions have largely to do with the image we have of God, the sort of God we conceive him to be. They are, in fact, theological questions. Perhaps you have said in the past, "Oh, I don't go in much for theology." But if you are a Christian believer, you have a theology. *Theology* means "God-talk." Every time you address God in prayer, receive Communion, or confess your sins, you are acting on the basis of your conceptions about the nature of God and human beings.

Your conception, the way you talk about God, is theology. When you read the Bible, the way you interpret it is part of your theology, because you interpret the Bible from a certain perspective. Obviously, in order to be able to talk to God, and to talk about him and your faith, you must be clear in your own mind about your personal theology. And, of course, a good place to begin is with your conception of God.

Faith is the *way* we believe; theology is the *content* of our beliefs. In this life we will never be able to understand God and his ways. His ways are above our ways. The human mind cannot encompass the many attributes of God. We have to be careful in our thinking about God not to limit him or seek to put him in a box. Even as I use the pronoun "he" in reference to God, I am limiting my conception of God to a certain extent. On the one hand, we should not imagine God in too-human terms, as a kind of Superman in the clouds somewhere, who has to be cajoled into answering our requests. On the other hand, we should not imagine God to be so big or abstract or unreachable that we forget that he is a personal God. He is the King, but he is also the Father, the Savior, the Comforter.

The doctrine of the Trinity, as difficult as it seems, can actually be a help in our understanding of God. The three persons of the Trinity—Father, Son, and Holy Spirit—could be seen as representing different activities of God and different responses of God to his children. In a sense we have a special relationship with each person of the Trinity. We may address God the Father, Jesus the Son, or the Holy Spirit at different times in our prayers, as it is appropriate. Let's look at the persons of the Trinity, and the role of each in our prayer life.

In the Name of Jesus

I will begin with the second person of the Trinity, Jesus Christ, because we pray not only to him but through him, in his name, and because he is our model in prayer. It is from

Jesus that we learn about prayer. The Bible represents prayer as the only activity Jesus expressly taught the disciples, at their request. He taught a new way to pray—not like the "hypocrites," not "piling up empty phrases," but with reverence and faith. He taught us how to pray for healing by his example, and for forgiveness, the coming of the kingdom, our daily needs, and deliverance from evil. He taught us how to pray with faith, "believing that it will be so." He invited us to pray in his name: "In very truth I tell you, if you ask the Father for anything in my name, he will give it to you. So far you have asked nothing in my name. Ask and you will receive, that your joy may be complete" (John 16:23-24). "If you dwell in me, and my words in you, ask what you will, and you shall have it. This is my Father's glory, that you may bear fruit in plenty and so be my disciples" (John 15:7-8). He showed us how to pray by his own prayer life. He gave us the Lord's Prayer, which is without rival in the devotional literature of the world.

The Lord's Prayer is a model prayer. It is a masterpiece of conciseness, the opposite of the prayers of those "who imagine that the more they say the more likely they are to be heard" (Matt. 6:7). The prayer begins with an important lesson: Jesus encourages us to address God as "Father." Everything good and loving and encouraging is in that address. Jesus did not teach us to pray "my" Father, but always "our" Father.

"Holy be your name" shows our intention that it shall be considered as holy among us. It casts the prayer in reverence. Names had an almost mystical significance to the Hebrews; to revere the name is to revere the person.

The petition "Your kingdom come" means that we are praying that God's kingly rule will be set up in our hearts, that he will have lordship over each of us as well as the rest of the human race. The kingdom is not a realm on earth, but the reign of God over the universe. The church is that group of believers to whom the kingdom of God has come, is coming, and will come. But God's kingdom is bigger than the church, and will at last include the world. I believe that healing is a sign of the kingdom and an evidence that it is coming.

"Your will be done" is another way of saying the same thing—that we may wish to do the will of God, participate in the present and immediate execution of his will. We ask that God's will be done "on earth as in heaven." This is an important petition to keep in mind when we are wrestling with problems with the ideas of prayer and healing; for if there is no sickness or grief in heaven, we can probably assume that it is not God's will that there be sickness and grief on earth. At the same time it reminds us that our theology is limited and that the will of God "on earth as in heaven" cannot be shrunk.

Only one petition in the Lord's Prayer has to do with physical need. "Give us today our daily bread" seems to be not so much a request that God supply our physical and bodily needs for the rest of our lives, as it is a statement that God will supply only our needs for the day, and no more. As with the manna in the wilderness, it seems to be God's way to want to provide us with only enough to get us through each day. I have so often thought how greedy I have been in wanting more than that. I think that he does this so that we may depend solely on him, and not on our savings account or stored-up treasures. We cannot find our security in stored-away "supplies" (whatever these may be), lest we forget we are children dependent on a Father in heaven who provides for us.

Forgiving others as God forgives us is central to the Christian life. The two go hand in hand: "If you forgive others the wrongs they have done, your heavenly Father will also forgive you; but if you do not forgive others, then the wrongs you have done will not be forgiven by your Father" (Matt. 6:14-15). Forgiving others and receiving forgiveness are central to inner healing. There can be no inner healing without forgiveness, because that is, in fact, what inner healing is. Forgiving others is part of the price all of us who want prayer to be effective have to pay.

"And do not bring us to the test" is a puzzling petition in light of the statement in a letter of James: "For God is untouched by evil, and does not himself tempt anyone" (James 1:13). But together with the next passage, "deliver us from the evil one," I think the petition is simply a request for protection and a confirmation of our intention to be wary of evil. The Lord's Prayer ends with a simple exclamation of praise and adoration.

We do not have very many records of the prayers of Jesus, aside from the Lord's Prayer. There is his high-priestly prayer, at or following the Last Supper, in which he prays to his Father to "glorify thy Son, that the Son may glorify thee" (John 17:1). That prayer is answered in the cross and resurrection. He also repeats the petition of the Lord's Prayer, "Keep them from the evil one" (John 17:15). There is his prayer at Gethsemane, in which he prayed, "My Father, if it is not possible for this cup to pass me by without my drinking it, thy will be done" (Matt. 26:42). In this prayer Jesus was struggling with that part of him, the natural part of him, that didn't want to suffer, be rejected, or die. I believe he was also expressing a dread of that hell into which he was to descend, the sins he was to take upon him. Yet there was a center in him that would do what God wanted no matter what. While he was willing to do God's will, he was bold enough to ask that he would not have to go through it; for he taught us to ask, since it is by asking that we receive. In this case—as in the case of James and John, who wanted to sit at Jesus' right and left hand—the request could not be granted; but there was no shame in asking.

Neither do we have many records of Jesus' prayers for healing. We do not hear the actual prayers, but we do hear the commands for demons to leave, that sins be forgiven, that the person be made well and rise. In no case does Jesus refuse to heal a person, saying that his sickness is "God's will." Later I will have more to say about Jesus' example in healing prayer.

If we do not have many examples of Jesus' actual prayers,

we do have clues about his prayer life, and we have many specific instructions from him about how to pray. We know that, after a day in which he healed many, "Very early next morning he got up and went out. He went away to a lonely spot and remained there in prayer" (Mark 1:35). We know that he urged his followers to have a "quiet time" as well; after the apostles returned from preaching and healing, "He said to them, 'Come with me, by yourselves, to some lonely place where you can rest quietly' " (Mark 6:31). We see Jesus going out in a boat to pray, going up on a mountain to pray, going out into a garden to pray. Yet he had enormous powers of abstraction and concentration, and could heal the sick and even raise the dead while surrounded by a noisy crowd. Luke tells us that it was while Jesus was praying following his baptism that the Holy Spirit descended on him (Luke 3:21-22). It seems that he truly prayed constantly and admonished his disciples (and us, his later disciples) to do so likewise (Luke 18:1-8).

Jesus' instructions on how to pray are specific, and useful. He told us, "In your prayers do not go babbling on like the heathen, who imagine that the more they say the more likely they are to be heard" (Matt. 6:7). In this we see that the value of prayer does not lie in the prayer itself, or in the one who is praying; eloquent prayers are not heard any more than simple ones. He taught us an enormous amount about the prayer of faith, repeating over and over in one way or another, "Whatever you pray for in faith you will receive" (Matt. 21:22). How can our prayer life fail to be exciting if we heed those words? He taught us to pray for all things with faith: "I tell you, then, whatever you ask for in prayer, believe that you have received it and it will be yours" (Mark 11:24). Jesus made clear the importance of forgiveness in prayer. "And when you stand praying, if you have a grievance against anyone, forgive him, so that your Father in heaven may forgive you the wrongs you have done" (Mark 11:25). Above all, he made clear his own role in prayer: as his children, we are to pray in his name; "If you ask anything in my name I will do it" (John 14:14). "If you ask the Father for anything in my name, he will give it you" (John 16:23). And it seems as though we naturally turn to Jesus in our prayers, especially in times of grief and distress, for he is the God-man; he suffered the same griefs and temptations we do; he is Friend as well as Savior. "Yet on himself he bore our sufferings, our torments he endured" (Isa. 53:4).

To a Loving Father

Jesus gave us what was in his time a new picture of a loving God. He taught us to call God "Abba"—Daddy. The first person of the Trinity is God, the Father and Creator. We address our requests in prayer to God the Father, through Jesus his son. From Jesus' words, we know that God is a loving Father, who loves to give to his children. God wants us to ask, wants us to trust him to be concerned about us. "For everyone who asks receives, he who seeks finds, and to him who knocks, the door will be opened" (Luke 11:10). "If you, then, bad as you are, know how to give your children what is good for them, how much more will the heavenly Father give the Holy Spirit to those who ask him!" (Luke 11:13). God is many times more loving than the most loving earthly father. He does not rebuke us for asking, as Jesus did not rebuke James or John, no matter how outrageous the request, if it is sincere. He wants us to have that kind of complete trust in him. He wants us to ask about the big and the small things. And we can rest assured that he will always give us what is good for us, better sometimes than what we asked for to begin with. Jesus showed us that nothing is too small or too great to bring to God in prayer, from reviving the dead and healing the sick, to providing a meal and calming stormy weather. Everything in our lives is a matter for prayer, unceasing prayer, even importunate prayer, like the widow pleading with the corrupt judge.

You may wonder why we should make our requests known to God when "your Father knows what your needs are before you ask him" (Matt. 6:8). I think that part of the reason we make our requests known is so that we may be clear in our own minds about what we desire. We must formulate our requests. The sons of Zebedee requested something through their mother that they really did not understand (Matt. 20:20-23). We should not, as Jesus advises, make our prayers long or repetitious, thinking that we will thereby convince God to do what we ask; he knows better than we what is best for us, and his will must be done. But we may sometimes need to pray at length or repeatedly in order to convince *ourselves*. When we pray requesting something, when we repeat a word or phrase in meditation, when we affirm something over and over, we may be doing so for our own benefit.

I think it is true in life as a whole, as well as prayer, that you get what you ask for. It is clear that the key to prayer is faith; these repetitions are the means of increasing our faith, by conscious efforts that affect our unconscious state. If we affirm faith by external words or actions, the meaning will sink into the unconscious and reemerge as authentic faith. It is sometimes difficult to believe that we can claim the promises Jesus made about answered prayer; then we may have to prepare ourselves to receive the good gifts. Jesus encouraged us to be persistent in prayer. It may also be that God is interested in seeing how earnest we are in our requests. Perhaps Jesus is saying that we should not be afraid to "trouble" God with our concerns.

We usually address our prayers of praise to God the Creator. The Psalms are full of praise for God and his creation. "The heavens tell out the glory of God, the vault of heaven reveals his handiwork" (Ps. 19:1). It is natural, as part of God's creation, to wish to praise him and his work. One of the great values of Christian meditation is the opportunity to meditate on the wonder of God's acts. We may enter into the timeless awe expressed by the Psalmist: "When I look up at thy heavens, the work of thy fingers, the moon and the stars set in their place by thee, what is man that thou shouldst remember him, mortal man that thou shouldst care for him?" (Psalm 8:3-4). The wonder is that God, who in the beginning created this world and all the universe, sustains it and cares for it still. And he cares for each person. God cares for each little bird; and "you are worth far more than the birds!" (Luke 12:24). God is just great enough to love each of us as his own child. This cannot be explained or understood, but for that matter neither can the love of an earthly father for his children really be explained. Praise and thanksgiving are the other side of the coin of prayer. Gratitude is the natural response of love. When we praise and thank God, we are "giving" to him; and it is such a small thing, really.

Filled with the Spirit

The best gift God has to give us is his Holy Spirit—the Comforter, the Counselor, the third person of the Trinity. The doctrine of the Holy Spirit has been one of the most neglected and abused doctrines of the church. In the traditional church the Holy Spirit has been sadly neglected; in some contemporary churches he has been too centralized. Some churches seem afraid of the movement of the Holy Spirit in the congregation; others preach a requisite "second baptism" in the Holy Spirit.

I think that the phrase "baptism of the Holy Spirit" is a misnomer. I would prefer to call the experience of God's life-giving power within us by another name—release of the Holy Spirit, infilling of the Holy Spirit, and so forth—to avoid confusion. We preach "one Lord, one faith, one baptism; one God and Father of all, who is over all and through all and in all" (Eph. 4:5-6). We are baptized in the name of the Father, Son, *and* Holy Spirit. To speak of a second baptism sounds to me as if God had a hidden agenda—the first Baptism somehow wasn't enough, so we must try again. That there is a very real experience of infilling or release I do not doubt for a minute. But filling with the Holy Spirit is ongoing, not a onetime event. I was baptized in the Holy Spirit when I was one month old. I have experienced infilling many times.

Neither should "praying in tongues" be taken as a sure or necessary sign of being filled with the Holy Spirit. You will notice that speaking in tongues is not one of the fruits of the Spirit listed in Gal. 5:22-23. But it is one of many gifts that Christians may receive, and, as Paul makes very plain, it is neither more nor less important than others. While we should not "forbid ecstatic utterance" (1 Cor. 14:39), it is certainly not a requisite of the Christian life or the Christian prayer-response. Don't feel like a second-class citizen if you don't speak in tongues. To call some Christians "charismatic" because they speak in tongues is to exclude other "gifted ones." All Christians have the *charismata,* gifts to be used to build up the body of Christ.

The Spirit shows himself in both dramatic and subtle ways. Some are granted speaking in tongues, being "slain in the spirit," sights of angels, visions, prophecies, and other such dramatic manifestations of the Spirit. But these experiences are accessories to, and not the basis of, the faith. "You are not disqualified by the decision of people who go in for self-mortification and angel-worship, and try to enter into some vision of their own" (Col. 2:18). But seek the Holy Spirit, and having asked for him, thank God that you have already received him. God desires to give of his very self to you, just as a parent's greatest gift to a child is not presents but himself. The Holy Spirit is one gift that God never refuses, never delays in giving. He delights in giving us this best of all gifts.

Living in the Spirit of God is a daily process. Pray daily the prayer of Psalm 51:10-12: "Create a pure heart in me, O God, and give me a new and steadfast spirit; do not drive me from thy presence or take thy holy spirit from me; revive in me the joy of thy deliverance and grant me a willing spirit to uphold me." What if you don't "feel" anything? Remember that "the harvest of the Spirit is love, joy, peace, patience, goodness, fidelity, gentleness, and self-control" (Gal. 5:22). The Holy Spirit is our teacher; he convicts us of sin; he intercedes for us in prayer when we do not ourselves know how to pray; he is our source of power. The Holy Spirit is God at work in our daily lives and the present world. He is the great go-between. In the power of the Holy Spirit we heal, teach, and preach. The power of the Holy Spirit enables us to do the impossible. One of the prayers I pray daily is a form of the Jesus Prayer most helpful to me: "Lord Jesus Christ, Son of God, fill me with the power of your love and the glory of your humility." In meditation we can "connect up" with the Holy Spirit of God. After meditation many people find themselves bursting with energy and creativity. God has promised the Holy Spirit to us; we need only ask to claim that promise. "But you will receive power when the Holy Spirit comes upon you" (Acts 1:8).

Evil

While we are talking and thinking about God, it is only natural to wonder about the devil and demons. I see "Satan" or "the Devil" or "the Evil One" as not necessarily literal representations of the power of evil; the reality cannot, of course, be contained in mere words. The words are windows which show us the dark side of reality. It is a relational, personal way of expressing the malignancy of evil. The biblical picture of "Satan" as a fallen angel and surrounded by other fallen angels (demons) is a way of talking about the radicalness, the willfulness of evil. It is the story of the Fall. Evil is not just a neutral or abstract force. The only way we can express the horror of evil—opposition to God—is to see it as a force which is personal in nature. This personal force, which we call Satan, is a liar and seeks to oppose, destroy, and frustrate God's purposes. I think that when we speak of demons, we are speaking of the personal, specific effects of evil in our lives.

I think that too many Christians today seek to place blame on Satan, or on demons, for every bad thing that happens, from accidents to personal failings, and so try to escape their own *responsibility* to God. C. S. Lewis said, "There are two equal and opposite errors into which our race can fall about devils. One is to disbelieve in their existence. The other is to believe, to have an excessive and unhealthy interest in them." "Demon possession" is being blamed today for everything from schizophrenia to smoking. I don't think that I have seen more than two or three people whom I would call "demon-possessed." I see these people as having been "taken over" by a complex to the degree that they have no control over themselves any longer. For example, anger can become such a habitual form of behavior that it becomes entrenched in a person and develops a life of its own. It makes a home for itself, and controls the person rather than the other way around.

This sort of entrenchment can be recognized by the sense you get of darkness in the person. If you should ever encounter this sort of problem, the complex must be addressed directly in Jesus' name. Remember that there is no biblical precedent for sending "demons" or "spirits" to hell, for we do not know whether that is where they belong. The safest course is to send them to Jesus, who will deal with them in his own way.

However, cases of "demon possession" are few and far between. It is a mistake to think that any habit or problem which we find difficult to control is the result of demon possession. We are by nature in bondage to sin. We are in bondage to our own sinful nature; our own rebelliousness makes our faults difficult to control. Even St. Paul said, "What I do is not what I want to do, but what I detest" (Rom. 7:15). But we would not say that Paul was demon-possessed. It is, in fact, dangerous to suggest the possibility of demon possession to a suffering person. If they bring it up, you should examine the possibility; but otherwise mentioning it will probably do more harm than good. I knew of a young boy suffering from schizophrenia who killed himself after it was suggested to him that he was demon-possessed.

Probably the only advantage in praying for someone "as if" he is demon-possessed is the *command* aspect of such prayer. I think this would probably account for the success of many "deliverance" ministries. Many people when praying are uncertain and wavering, but find that if they can address something as concrete as a "demon" and command it to leave, their prayers are much more firm and convincing. It is possible, however, to do this command sort of prayer without bringing demonism into it. When praying for the mentally ill, I often address a disturbing emotion, such as fear, by name, commanding it to leave the person in Jesus' name. Such a prayer of unwavering certainty has beneficial effects, both as prayer and in the unconscious mind of the person being prayed for. Jesus took advantage of this when he prayed for the mentally ill, who in his time were probably all thought to be demon-possessed.

The important thing to remember is that the Evil One is *already a defeated enemy*. He has already lost the war. God triumphed on the cross. "If God is on our side, who is against us?" (Rom. 8:31). Sin and death, the sum of evil, were conquered on the cross. "In the same way you must regard yourselves as dead to sin and alive to God, in union with Christ Jesus" (Rom. 6:11). We *are* God's children. Nothing can take that away from us.

3

FAITH AND PRAYER

"Do not be afraid; only have faith" (Mark 5:36). That is the basic word of Jesus for every human being in every age. That's how Jesus lived—with faith and without fear; and that is the program for all of us who claim in any way to be his followers. Jesus was talking about something that is as real for us as it was for the anxious father of the little girl in the story in which these words are found. In some ways we know more about the universe and the way it works now than did the people of Jesus' time, but that knowledge has not reduced our fears. As we grow up, we discard some of the fears of childhood, only to discover that greater understanding and information and wider responsibilities can enlarge the area of our fears. A child may be afraid of a shadow cast on the wall by a flickering light, but knows nothing of the shadows cast on the adult mind by the real dangers that threaten our welfare or our very existence, or the ultimate fears that hover over our sophisticated society—our fears that life makes no sense, that it has no direction or meaning, and that death is oblivion.

Faith Is the Key

How difficult it is to become like children. Yet this is exactly what is asked of us in prayer. Jesus tells us that faith—*believing that it shall be so*—is the key to answers in prayer. Even prayers of praise and thanksgiving and meditation require faith—faith that we have been heard, faith even in the existence of the living God. Faith is, of course, a gift. It is not something one can work for or work up. It is a gift from God, for "no one can say 'Jesus is Lord!' except under the influence of the Holy Spirit" (1 Cor. 12:3). But it is a gift we can cultivate—by asking for it in prayer and by preparing ourselves to receive it. It is my experience that it increases unobtrusively.

According to Heb. 11:1, faith "gives substance to our hopes, and makes us certain of realities we do not see." Obviously, anything that we have proof of is no longer held in faith, but in knowledge. It is easy to believe in what you have proof of; but it takes a radical trust to believe a promise for which you have no proof. "Happy are they who never saw me and yet have found faith" said Jesus (John 20:29). We have no *proof* of the validity of the Christian faith. We do have *evidence*, however. We have the historical fact of Jesus of Nazareth and the promises of the Bible; we have the history of the Christian church; we have our own inner convictions. These impel us toward belief. But faith—actually believing the seemingly impossible, that a man who died on a hill outside of Jerusalem was God, that he was resurrected from the dead by the power of God's Holy Spirit, that he has ascended, bringing our very flesh into heaven, and that it makes a difference in our lives—is a gift from God. Likewise, believing that through prayer a difficult-to-cure disease is going to get better can only be a gift from God.

How do we receive the gift of faith? All Christians have faith and can learn to recognize it; we can also ask for its increase. The disciples asked Jesus to increase their faith; in a growing prayer life it is one of the first things to ask for in prayer, because it is so absolutely necessary in prayer. Jesus said, "Have faith in God. I tell you this: if anyone says to this mountain, 'Be lifted from your place and hurled into the sea,' and has no inward doubts, but believes that what he says is happening, it will be done for him. I tell you, then, whatever you ask for in prayer, believe that you have received it and it will be yours" (Mark 11:22-24). Clearly, all things are possible with God, and through faith the power of God is available to us.

So great is the power of belief that it can be used wrongly. Many non-Christians have received healing and "success" through the use of "positive thinking" techniques. There is no denying that such secular use of belief often works. The question to ask is not whether it really works but whether it is right. Therefore, before you embark on a campaign of prayer and affirmation regarding a request, test it to see if it is within God's will. Is it in accord with God's Word? No behavior should ever contradict his will as revealed in his Word and a Spirit-inspired conscience. We can be fairly sure about some things; increased faith, healing of illness, increase of the Holy Spirit, someone's salvation, forgiveness of sins, and material provision can be assumed to be God's will. But a raise in salary, a particular house, or a particular job are not quite as certain. If, after filtering your request through God's will as revealed in the Bible and your conscience, you still have no clear picture, go ahead and pray with faith anyway. God wants to hear your requests. But pray for guidance as well. This is the time to add "Your will be done" to your prayers, as Jesus did in Gethsemane. The important thing is your prayerful attitude about faith—your willingness to subject the power of belief to the will of God, the author of all belief.

When you are fairly sure you can proceed with your prayer, you should go ahead with full confidence, making every effort to develop faith. "But he must ask in faith, without a doubt in his mind; for the doubter is like a heaving sea ruffled by the wind. A man of that kind must not expect the Lord to give him anything; he is double-minded, and never can keep a steady course" (James 1:6-8). God wants to know that you are sure and sincere. "No one who sets his hand to the plough and then keeps looking back is fit for the kingdom of God" (Luke 9:62). I have learned to discipline my mind not to accept doubt and fear, because they often work exactly the opposite of faith. Faith is absolutely essential to prayer. Many times Jesus bemoaned the disciples' lack of faith—when they were afraid of a storm, or when they were unable to heal a sick person, for example. Before healing the blind men, Jesus asked them, "'Do you believe that I have the power to do what you want?'" When they responded that they did, he said, "'As you have believed, so let it be'" (Matt. 9:28-29). To many of those he healed, he said, "Your faith has made you well" (Matt. 9:2, 22, 15:28; Mark 2:5, 5:34, 10:52; Luke 5:20, 7:50, 8:48, 17:19, 18:42).

In faith we become like children. Faith—believing in the impossible, or believing against the evidence in things we cannot see—involves the kind of trust children have in their mother or father or a beloved friend, the kind of person they can turn to in a crisis. At the center of our faith, at the center of all the creeds and church structure, is a person, Jesus, to whom we can turn with that kind of trust. There is no one way to express that trust, for we are all different. But there is, I believe, no single human being who is excluded by temperament or training from that trust, which is faith.

In the fifth chapter of Mark we see two very different people respond in faith to Jesus. I see Jairus as the intellectual, the president of one of the synagogues, trained in the Hebrew Scriptures—the last person in many ways one would expect to be attracted to the unconventional young preacher from Nazareth. Yet at a point in deep human need, with his daughter mortally ill, Jairus responded not as an intellectual or important person, but as a desperately distressed father. Nothing else mattered–not his temperament, his training, his prejudices, his prestige. He was just a human being in need, letting his heart speak as Jesus drew from him a deep and unexpected trust.

On the other hand, the woman in the crowd I see as a totally different personality–ignorant, perhaps slightly hysterical, shriveled in body and soul by years of hemorrhaging. For her there was no confrontation with Jesus, no prejudice to overcome. She acted impulsively. She didn't believe she was important enough to talk to Jesus. She knew nothing save her instinct that in him was the power of God. So her act of trust found expression not in words, but in nothing more than a gesture. She simply touched his cloak. That was all. That was enough, enough to make Jesus stop, "aware that power had gone out of him" (Mark 5:30). Her faith had cured her.

Desperate need is often enough to bring faith. What we need desperately to believe, we will believe. But many times we are too discouraged or too skeptical to believe, or our need is not so great, allowing our reason to plague us with doubts. In most cases, we must begin with the great prayer, "Help me where faith falls short" (Mark 9:24). You cannot go on entertaining those doubts. Many people complain that they can't help their negative cast of mind. But there are, in fact, ways to push away negative thoughts and increase faith.

The Power of Affirmation

I have found that affirmation and visualization are great aids in increasing faith. *Can'ts* are all poison words. Every time you say "I can't do it," or "It can't happen," you assure "Junior," as Agnes Sanford calls your unconscious mind, of that impossibility. Saying "I can't remember names," "I can't get well," "I can't quit smoking" are sure ways of making sure that you never will. You get what you ask for and expect. Psychology knows that the way to change those *can'ts* into *cans* is to say "I can" each morning and each evening—one hour after you get up and within one hour before you go to bed. By repeating a "can," in a few weeks to a month you will have convinced your unconscious mind that it can happen. You may feel ridiculous saying something which you believe to be impossible or untrue. But if you can get over that initial barrier, you will find your feelings changing.

This is affirmation. Affirmations are a kind of prayer. I would put affirmations into the category of positive confession. It is powerful to hear something, whether positive or negative. Affirmations show our desire to confess the will and word of God, stated in words that are our own, to build them into our own psyche and hence influence our behavior. I see affirmations, and the intentions behind them, as a way of changing attitudes. An attitude change always causes behavior changes. Attitudes even alter facts. I believe that reciting the great creeds of the church aloud each week in church, and even oftener, will have a powerful effect on the unconscious mind. "For the faith that leads to righteousness is in the heart, and the confession that leads to salvation is upon the lips" (Rom. 10:10). (It is important to remember that the way we think of the mind [the seat of thought] and the heart [the seat of feeling] is not the way the Hebrews thought of them. *Heart* to the Hebrews meant the *inner person,* what we call the unconscious—the inner person which God moves.) Constant affirmation is part of constant prayer.

The Bible is full of affirmations. "All that is true, all that is noble, all that is just and pure, all that is lovable and gracious, whatever is excellent and admirable—fill your thoughts with these things" (Phil. 4:8). "Be always joyful; pray continually; give thanks whatever happens; for this is what God in Christ wills for you" (1 Thess. 5:16-18). Repeating a Bible verse over and over is a powerful kind of affirmation. It gets deep into the deepest layers of the mind, where it can and does affect attitude and as a result behavior.

In affirmation we believe that we have already received our request, even if there are not yet any results. Sometimes we believe against the evidence. We discipline our minds to refuse doubt. For example, you might say, "I enjoy weighing 120 pounds, and I eat all the right foods to stay at that weight," "I enjoy working in a job that is just right for me," and so on. It may help to thank God that you have already received it: "Thank you, Lord, that my broken leg is already beginning to mend," "Thank you that my lost dog is on his way home right now." The more immediate the affirmation is, the better: "Thank you that this is happening right now." It takes courage and unwavering faith to say that something is happening when you have no evidence that it is. But when you do not leave yourself an out, when you can't cover yourself, you cannot help believing.

It is important in affirmation to be as positive as possible, even in the way you word your affirmations. "Junior," your unconscious mind, is extremely capricious. If you say, "I hope I don't get sick," he will pick up on the word "sick" and you may end up with the opposite result from what you intended. Affirm the positive: "I'm glad I'm in perfect health." Be as concrete as you can. "Thank you, God, that I am in perfect health and full of energy and joy." God can work through "Junior," who controls the operation of your body and gives rise to your conscious thoughts. Junior gets these messages, and by the power of God he sends out signals to the body to heal itself or fight disease, or to the mind to increase its efficiency or creativity.

Using Visualization

Visualization can be a powerful affirmative tool. If you want to lose weight, your diet will go more easily if you can affirm your desired weight and, as often as you can, visualize yourself at that weight. See yourself in a new wardrobe looking delightfully thin. Visualize yourself in a new job, getting along with your spouse, with your leg healed, or whatever. Create a picture in great detail. Relish it. Your unconscious mind will try to match the picture you hold before it. Somehow we have come to think of the unconscious mind as mysteriously untouchable and beyond our use. I do not think this is realistic. Your imagination is a faculty to be respected and used. God can speak to you through your imagination.

St. Paul declared, "I have strength for anything through him who gives me power" (Phil. 4:13). Nothing is impossible to God. Dare to hope for the impossible. It is a great risk, but one with great rewards. Instead of complaining about obstacles, find ways to make things happen. God created the laws of nature, and he can work through nature. A miracle is not something contrary to nature but something which is contrary to what we have *observed* about nature. It is not a violation of nature, but an unusual use of nature's laws. "Miraculous" healings may simply involve the healing abilities of the body itself, either speeded up or strengthened. God may simply cut short the healing process. Miracles are possible every day. God can use your mind, your imagination, and your body to work his miracles. We only have to be ready; to have faith, without fear.

4

PRAYER AND HEALING

Jesus said, "Give, and gifts will be given you. Good measure, pressed down, shaken together, and running over, will be poured into your lap; for whatever measure you deal out to others will be dealt to you in return" (Luke 6:38). We can grow only so far in our prayer life before the next natural step is sharing what we have received, thereby opening new doors for growth. Do not be surprised if, as your prayer life grows, you are asked to pray for someone, especially for healing.

We pray for people for the same reason Jesus prayed for people—because we love them. Like his Father, Jesus loves us and does not want to see us suffer. We do not hear of Jesus ever refusing to heal someone. Healing was a vitally important part of his ministry, together with preaching and teaching. Nearly one-fifth of the Gospels is devoted to discussion of Jesus' healings. There are 41 instances of physical and mental healings mentioned in the Gospels. And, as we can see by the book of Acts, his disciples carried out his command to continue his healing work.

The Healing Ministry of Jesus

The healing ministry of Jesus made his teachings concrete; what better way is there to show love and concern than to cure physical and emotional ills? Jesus himself indicated that his healings were a sign of the coming of the kingdom of God. He healed primarily because he had compassion—the word means, literally, "suffering together." As God incarnate, his love reached out in a caring, healing ministry. Jesus was so committed to healing that he even broke the Sabbath laws in order to heal. Many of his healings involved a simple command for a demon to leave or for a part to be made whole; several times he linked forgiveness of sins to healing; often he indicated that the person's faith made him whole. Jesus is our example in healing. It is on his command, and by his promise, that we pray for the sick and the broken.

We have several detailed examples of Jesus' way of healing. One is contained in Mark 9. In this incident Christ, coming down off the mountain with Peter, James, and John, found the disciples and the scribes arguing in the midst of a crowd. They were arguing about the case of a "demon-possessed" or epileptic boy whom the disciples were unable to help. One can imagine the disciples and the scribes, like a group of modern doctors or professors, discussing the diagnosis and modes of treatment. They were trying to use their humanity to help. But as St. Augustine said, "I found in my studies of Plato and Cicero many fine things acutely said; but in none of them did I find 'Come unto Me and rest.' "

Only Jesus could take the proper action: "Bring him to me."

The father brought the child, saying, "If it is at all possible for you, take pity upon us and help us." This shows the solidarity of sorrow—not pity just on the boy, but on father and son together.

Jesus zeroed in on the words "if" and "possible." "Everything is possible to one who has faith" (Mark 9:22). This is his challenge to a doubting church. The father's request speaks for us all. Life is a mixture of belief and unbelief. He was saying, "Don't let my lack of faith decide. Let your grace alone decide."

When the boy was healed, the disciples had to ask, "Why could not we cast it out?" (v. 28). Jesus' response was, "There is no means of casting out this sort but prayer" (v. 29). Some versions add "and fasting." We can see that Christ varied his approach from person to person, discerning how best to approach the problem.

Fasting speaks of a deep truth. It is an example of the self-discipline, hard training, and spiritual exercise of discipleship. It is uncompromising. There is no special merit in fasting; in fact, for people suffering from depression it may be the worst thing to do. Nevertheless, the Christian must be willing to do what is asked of him. He is a spiritual athlete under the discipline of the divine captain. We must be willing to sacrifice ourselves, to let the divine into the situation, eschewing human motives and methods. But the emphasis here is that this epilepsy or demon possession comes out not by command but by prayer. I think Jesus was gently urging the disciples to follow his example of constant prayer and meditation so that the power of love would be increased in each of them.

In Mark 8 we see Jesus using a different approach. In this case a blind man was brought to him. Instead of healing him before the crowd, Jesus "took the blind man by the hand and led him away out of the village" (v. 23). This was a departure from Christ's customary methods. Some commentators say he handled this man differently to display his power, to show that he didn't have to tie himself to a single method, but could choose different methods to show his liberty and power. But Christ was free in everything; he didn't need to prove it. The commentators' argument implies that Jesus was more intent on teaching abstract doctrines than on bringing his healing power to people. I believe he operated differently simply because this particular case called for it.

Jesus took the man's hand, left the crowds, left the sufferer's friends, left the disciples. He led him through the streets and pathways, out into the fields, for perfect privacy. We can see Christ's strong sympathy and his intention to heal. If you have ever helped a blind person, you will have a feeling of kinship with Christ in this regard. The great love of Bethlehem and Calvary is here: he has taken us all by the hand. Why didn't Jeus tell the man's friends to take him? Jesus wasn't especially interested in giving orders; he was interested in acting out the message himself. He gives the personal touch.

Christ perceived that this was the way to help the man. The blind man was helpless, confused, dull, unexpectant, crushed. How was aid to reach him? How was his poor battered spirit to be aroused? Words might be futile; a loving glance would surely be lost on him. But when he felt his hand taken, his heart must have been stirred. He began to feel less lonely. Hope began to spring up. The touch of a hand touched his heart, too, and it thawed the icy barriers. It was an acted-out parable of the incarnation of God in Jesus Christ. God comes to us with a personal touch; we are touched by God's Son, our Savior.

Before commencing the cure, Christ brought the man into isolation. This business could only be done face to face. Hasn't Christ isolated us to cure us, too? Often we are so busy that we keep him at arm's length. Sometimes he allows solitude to come to us in the form of illness, an enforced rest, the loss of a job. Jesus means to have us to himself. He wants to speak to us alone. He wants us to listen and to receive.

Jesus used material signs in healing to help the mind accept what was happening. Jesus didn't have to use the repeated touch, the application of saliva, but he used them in this case. His aim was to help the blind man to trust him. Jesus doesn't make things complicated. He uses simple tools. He used sense and matter because a sense-bound nature could be helped that way. He wrapped the divine actions in commonplace envelopes. Jesus addresses us in words and ways that suit our capacity. Jesus was body, mind, and spirit, because we are body, mind, and spirit. God deals with us as Jesus dealt with the blind man. He puts his message of love into a human life and death. The bread and wine of Communion are a living reminder of the really present, loving Lord.

Jesus healed the man by stages. After one touch, he asked the man whether he felt any better, like any doctor; he then reapplied the remedy tool. Jesus was adjusting the speed of the operation to the man's weakened faculty of trust. He is a patient God and a patient Savior. Jesus wanted to take the blind man beyond seeing only with his eyes to seeing with his heart. The man emerged from this encounter not only with new eyesight, but with a renewed sense of trust and hope and love.

This is a model for our praying for others. Like Jesus, we must look at and listen to the suffering person. We must suit our approach to his needs; we must seek to help the whole person, body, mind, and spirit.

The Holistic View

When we pray for healing we make use of the *holistic* view; that is, we see the human being as a union of body, spirit, mind, emotions, and will. The dichotomy in western thought between soul and body, in which the body is seen as a hindrance to the immortal soul, is largely the result of Greek influences. In the Hebrew tradition, no such dichotomy existed. The Hebrews had no distinct words for what the Greeks called the *psyche* (mind and emotions), *soma* (body), and *pneuma* (spirit). They saw these components of human beings as interdependent and equally blessed. As we can see by his healings, Jesus continued in this tradition; he often forgave sins while producing physical healings. I believe that the holistic view is the view most authentic to Christianity. We do not believe in the Greek notion of the immortality of the soul, but in the resurrection of body and spirit alike. Paul says that we will be raised, not as disembodied spirits, but as a "spiritual body" (1 Cor. 15:44)—imperishable, perfect. We remember the unity of body and spirit when we receive Communion.

The philosophical separation of body, mind, and spirit has taken its toll on western medicine. Modern medicine often views disease as being caused only by external factors, having nothing to do with a person's mental or emotional state. It sees the body as the territory of medical doctors, the mind as the province of psychiatrists or psychologists, and the spirit as the specialty of ministers.

Recent studies are proving the error of this division, and support the intimate relationship between mind and matter. One of the most significant discoveries of recent years is that cardiovascular disease is many times more likely to occur in a person who has what is called a Type A personality—aggressive, impatient, short-tempered, hard-driving—than in a Type B person, who is more easygoing. It has been found also that people who repress unpleasant emotions run a greater risk of developing some forms of cancer than other people. And it has been known for some time that ailments such as migraine headaches and asthma are related to emotional stress. Doctors have called such ailments *psychosomatic* illnesses—that is, showing a relationship between *psyche* (mind and emotions) and *soma* (body). We can venture to say that almost all disease is psychosomatic or psychogenic, whether obviously or subtly, because illness always affects the whole person.

Fortunately, the holistic approach is being revived today. Unfortunately, it has acquired a sometimes faddish aspect, and the spiritual element has been somewhat lost. Holistic medicine recognizes the problems resulting from a separation of mind and body, but its practitioners often do not recognize that the mind–body relationship is integrally related to religious faith. The mind is no substitute for the spirit.

For the holistic approach to be truly holistic, it must accept our spiritual needs. Christianity affirms the worth of the individual, as a creation of God. It is this worth which makes health and wholeness possible. It is no accident that the words *whole, health,* and *holy* are related. If we heal a person's body without healing their mind and spirit, they will only become ill again, perhaps unto death, for "it is better for you to enter into life maimed than to keep both hands and go to hell and the unquenchable fire" (Mark 9:43).

Keep the holistic view of human beings in mind when you pray for someone. Before praying for a physical ailment, question whether it might not be a symptom of a deeper problem—some locked-up pain, a troubled childhood, a stressful work situation or relationship, a grudge, guilt. Pray for the root problem as well as for the symptoms. Pray for the whole person.

Beginning to Pray for Healing

Beginning to pray for people is scary. You may feel flustered and awkward. It gets easier with experience. You may have people ask you to pray for them, especially family members, or you may feel called to offer to pray for someone. Either way, do not refuse them, unless you receive guidance of some sort not to. For example, an 85-year-old who is full of cancer and ready to die may not be a candidate for prayer for healing, but could use prayer for a good death.

This is an extremely delicate question, and one must use great discernment. It seems to be hard for me to pray for healing for five-year-olds with life-threatening illnesses, for example, unless I feel directed to do so. I often think they might be saved from something if they were to die. Some very ill people are ready to die and only need "permission" or a blessing to do so. Often the ill person has been brought by well-meaning relatives, but will be able to tell you that he or she is ready for and expecting death. There might be other reasons for feeling that you cannot pray for someone—if they have been brought to you under false pretenses, if they are hostile, and so on. It is a good idea to pray about it before you agree or offer to pray for someone. If you receive no guidance not to pray—as will probably happen—then go ahead and pray. When I receive the go-ahead signal, I will plunge with faith into the prayer.

I think all Christians should pray for people. Certain people may be gifted in praying, through practice, talent, or gift, but they are exceptions. Most of us have enough natural ability and faith to become rather able pray-ers. I do not feel that I have any gift of healing. I often "know" that people will be healed, but it is the knowledge of faith and not some special intuitive knowing. Most of the time I know because it is something I've seen healed before.

Faith seems necessary for healing to come about. I think that the chief need for faith is with the pray-er. The pray-er needs to be the one who carries the ball. Often the one who is prayed for is just too discouraged to have faith. It is very unwise to expect people who are seriously ill to have faith. That's why you must have faith *for* the person. "Simon, Simon, take heed: Satan has been given leave to sift all of you like wheat; but for you I have prayed that your faith may not fail; and when you have come to yourself, you must lend strength to your brothers" (Luke 22:31-32).

Of course, the very best circumstance is one in which both the pray-er and the one prayed for have faith that the prayer "shall be so," because then the two are agreed and united. Two may be exactly twice as strong as one. Just the fact that one has asked for or agreed to prayer is a sign of faith; it is sometimes better that they have just this little bit of faith than that they be overflowing with unrealistic expectations. Part of the purpose of prayer is the upbuilding of faith, which is why we rely on visualization so much: it makes a strong impression on the mind and heart.

The importance of the faith of the pray-er is one reason why it is so difficult to pray for yourself. Especially if you are discouraged, it is difficult to have faith that what seems impossible will be so. Also it is hard to discover the cause of your illness on your own. Self-healing prayer tends to focus on the problem, instead of the solution, to look inward rather than outward, and only makes things worse. We need each other. Sometimes if someone else has prayed for you and the problem isn't too bad you can take over for yourself. But generally it is a good idea to have someone else lift you out of yourself.

As important as the faith of the one praying is the willingness of the sick person to be made well. Believe it or not, many people are, unconsciously, not willing to give up their illness. When you think about it, being ill can be a fairly easy way of life. You are fed and clothed, get plenty of attention, and don't have to work or go to school. I say this at the risk of sounding callous; but it is an important truth. Some ill people realize that if they get well they will have to go to work or take other responsibility. There are also people, made ill by a long-standing grudge which consumes from the inside out, who may be unwilling to admit to or give up the grudge through forgiveness, which should be the first step toward healing. It is interesting that when Jesus came upon a man who had been ill and idle for 38 years, the first thing he asked him was, "Do you want to recover?" (John 5:7). You will have a difficult time praying for anyone who does not want to accept the responsibilities that go along with wholeness.

The Importance of Listening

When you have determined to your own satisfaction that you should pray for a person, and that they are ready to be made well, then you should decide how to pray, and what to pray for. You must take the time to sit and listen to the person explain what his or her ailment is, how they feel about it, what they hope for. This listening is not counseling; you are not going to try to solve the person's problems on your own. Stay away from advice-giving. You are there only to be a vehicle for God's healing power and comfort. In prayer you must put yourself in the background. If you allow your own personality and preferences to intrude and do not allow God to take over the reins, you will become far too drained and exhausted.

Whenever I pray for someone, I always listen very carefully before I utter a word of prayer. I ask the person whether they have seen a doctor, and what the doctor said. I will not see a person in lieu of their seeing a medical doctor, but only in addition to it, either before or after. If they have gone to a doctor, I need to know the diagnosis, what medicines are being taken, what the status of the disease and the prognosis are. The more concrete the information, the better.

After hearing what the medical screening has revealed, I am ready to listen for possible sources of the illness within the total human being. Is the person under terrible stress now? Have they been under it for any length of time? What is the stress about? Is it something they can avoid? Is the illness something they have had before? Is it chronic? How long have they had it? Is it hereditary? Are there any bad memories? Unresolved conflicts? Areas of unforgiveness? I am apt to ask questions about relations to family members, marriage, work, and childhood. I am interested in the person's religious training and understanding, though I generally veil any overt questions on the subject. This is not the time to proselytize, but only to love, to listen, and to pray.

After listening for sometimes an hour or more, if the time is available, with one ear open to God's guidance and one ear open to the person, I am ready to pray. As I have prayerfully listened, I have been forming a picture in my mind of what it is I am to pray about. I ask myself or sometimes even the person what the illness is saying to them.

The Healing Touch

When you have an idea of what to pray for, you can begin. Here is where prayer for healing differs from the kind of prayer you were probably brought up with. We were raised to pray *about* people, but not to pray *with* them or *for* them, which is more intimate. In praying for healing we pray as Jesus did, with the laying-on of hands. This simply means that throughout the prayer you maintain physical contact with the person you are praying for, usually by gently resting your hands on their shoulders or head, or on the afflicted part. The laying-on of hands accomplishes three things, I think. It follows biblical precedent. It has a psychological effect, being an expression of love, intimacy, and caring. And it is a contact point for the healing power of God to come in. Touching increases faith. It is sense-able. It gets the pray-er in touch with the one prayed for at his or her point of need.

It helps to imagine the healing power of God as being like electricity. It is always around, but we need to "turn it on" to be able to use it. Prayer in faith, using touch, gives the healing power a way to enter people. The importance of this personal contact is one reason why it is so difficult to pray from a distance or without the subject's knowing it. You do not have the benefit of touch or of the person's unconscious actually hearing the prayer. It is difficult to be an effective channel for God's love in this way. There are times when it is absolutely necessary to pray for someone at a distance, but it is not the best way. I would rather have someone who is with the person pray for them if possible.

When we speak of the "healing light" we are making use of the biblical imagery of the light of God and light of the world, and we are also referring to God's being the source of all energy. Scientists have found that everything, from matter to light to heat, is composed of energy; we may say that pure energy is "uncreated" energy. The light of God is his own life. When that energy or power enters into a person, we may visualize it as light. Some people find that they feel a sensation of heat when hands are laid on them in prayer, like radiation. This sensation is purely ancillary to the healing process. I seldom feel anything when I pray for a person, though they often testify that they do. But it shows the real quality of the light of God. Laying hands on a person, and visualizing in prayer the energy or light or healing power of God passing through you into the person you are praying for, is a good way of making concrete and believable the divine reality of healing in prayer.

It is interesting that now medical researchers have found that passing an electric current through hard-to-mend broken bones can speed healing dramatically. This will come as no surprise to those who are experienced in praying for healing, for it is exactly what we do. It is good if you can surround the afflicted part, if there is one, with your hands. If you are praying for a heart problem, for example, you can place one hand on the person's chest and one on their back, sandwiching the heart area in between.

When I am ready to pray for someone, I have them sit in a comfortable chair. I stand behind them with my hands on their shoulders and only later on their head or injured part. You might wish to kneel behind the person, if you prefer. I have learned to be absolutely still for a while after putting my hands on the person's shoulders. I seek to put my own mind in a place of openness to God. I don't want to push my feeling or my picture of the disease on the person. I want to be as open as possible for God's guidance. It is as if I put my conscious mind in neutral and my heart or spirit in gear. "Put all your trust in the

Lord and do not rely on your own understanding. Think of him in all your ways, and he will smooth your path" (Prov. 3:5-6).

When I have received a picture or an idea about how to pray, I begin, but not before some preliminaries. Usually before plunging immediately into the prayer for the individual I praise God, bless God, invoke his presence, and ask him to fill the room with his glory or with his holy angels. I worship him with my hands still on the shoulders of the individual. It is only as I begin to pray for the person that my hands touch the person. (In the next chapters I will discuss more precisely how to pray for various ailments, using examples from my own experience.) After the prayer is over, I leave the room and allow the person to sit quietly for a few minutes.

It is a good idea not to pray for another person right after you have been prayed for yourself. You need to conserve that healing energy for your own healing, rather than giving it away immediately. In fact, we urge people not to talk at all immediately following the prayer. I also advise people I have prayed for not to broadcast any positive results of the prayer. In particular, I advise cancer patients who go into remission not to talk about their progress in public for two years. During the healing process, one is too vulnerable to be put under scrutiny, and if the expectations are too high, disappointment will be faith-shattering.

For the same reason, I do not keep lists or statistics on the people I have prayed for. "It is a wicked, godless generation that asks for a sign," said Jesus (Matt. 12:39). We can never have proof of healing or of what has brought about healing. Proof excludes faith. A danger in statistics is that one begins to think that what one has done brings about the healing. Another danger is in thinking that the only aim of prayer is physical or mental healing. While we rejoice when we learn of the return to health of someone we have prayed for, we must not put healing above the general welfare, especially spiritual, of the person. Not everyone who is prayed for is healed; but everyone receives a blessing.

What I have just given is a general guideline for praying for healing. There are many variations possible. Most prayers last thirty minutes to one hour. But in some cases, for example when a person is desperately or chronically ill, a "soaking prayer" of several hours' duration is more helpful. The idea is to soak the person in prayer and the power of God's love. This is best accomplished in a group, with members of the group taking turns praying. It is often helpful even with shorter prayers to have a group praying, since Jesus promised, "Again I tell you this: if two of you agree on earth about any request you have to make, that request will be granted by my heavenly Father. For where two or three have met together in my name, I am there among them" (Matt. 18:19-20). I believe that two who agree about something are twice as strong as one. That number increases with the number of people praying, up to a point. However, as the numbers increase, the possibility of agreement shrinks, so that large groups can become argumentative and unmanageable. It is best to stick to small, close groups. I also do not like to pray for anyone more than a few times. Although some people do need more prayer, there is a danger of the person becoming too dependent on a particular pray-er, instead of on God.

Healing prayer has a powerful effect on the unconscious mind. Any suggestions you make to it will be heard, which is why it is important to be as positive as possible. As God uses human organs for praise, prayer, witness, and work, so he uses the central human computer system in the healing process. Both illness and healing seem to be set off in the brain. I believe that often the healing power of God works through the brain rather than on the organ itself, so that correcting whatever is troubling the mind can bring healing all over the body.

The Healing of Memories

One of the most useful tools in prayer for healing is praying for the healing of memories. People are often held in bondage by past hurts and memories of unpleasant events or periods in their lives. Through prayer we can ask Jesus, who is not bound by time or space, to heal the memory. Rather than picturing Jesus going back to the event, I have learned to picture Jesus as having always been there, which is closer to the truth. He is always with us, but his grace is not always asked or allowed to come in.

So in prayer I will describe for the person a picture of Jesus standing by when the event occurred, loving the person and suffering with him, often even crying with the person in his or her pain, offering comfort and mending conflicts. Jesus can offer the love that a fearful or neglectful father or mother couldn't give; he can comfort and bring together an estranged husband and wife. The realization that Jesus was there takes all the sting out of the memory, so that, while the memory is still there, it no longer hurts, and no longer has any power over the person.

Forgiveness of sins is central in many prayers. We know that Jesus felt that the statements "Your sins are forgiven" and "You are healed" were virtually synonymous, as he showed in healing the paralytic who was brought to him. Some people need to be forgiven for past sins that are haunting them; others must forgive those who have injured them. Prayer for the healing of memories is really a form of forgiveness, since what is forgiven is washed clean and should no longer trouble us.

Sin can cause illness. By this, I do not mean that illness is necessarily punishment for sin, as Job's accusers thought. But illness can be a consequence of sin, just as pain is a consequence of cutting your finger. I don't think that all illness is caused by sin; but much of it comes because we are fallen or sinful. If Jesus taught us to pray that God's will be done on earth as in heaven, and if, as we believe, there is no suffering in heaven, then we may assume that illness was not a part of the original scheme of things.

We have no record of Jesus being sick. We flunked the test, but Jesus passed it for us with an A. "And by his scourging we are healed" (Isa. 53:5).

5

PRAYING FOR PHYSICAL HEALING

It may come as a surprise to you to hear that doctors have never healed anyone. While I am very much for the medical establishment, since through it my life has been saved a number of times, I know that the Bible declares that God "heals all [our] diseases" (Ps. 103:3 RSV).

I am also aware that there are many misconceptions regarding the medical establishment. One of them is the idea that somehow modern medicine can eventually eliminate all disease. That is simply not possible. That is a humanistic picture, not the biblical one; for to eliminate disease would be to eliminate the consequences of the Fall, our separation from the Life-giver, and that is not possible by human means. According to the medical establishment itself, medical science has not reduced the number of human illnesses, but rather they have grown. While infectious diseases may be reduced in number (largely due to advances in sanitation, some say), the number of psychogenic and stress-related diseases is on the increase.

It is therefore imperative that when we talk about praying

for physical illness, we realize that medical science and prayer must be linked together, and that one of the main reasons that people ever get well through medical attention, both Christians and non-Christians, is because someone is praying for them. Even people in the public eye, like performers and political figures, who may have indicated by their life and words that they do not believe in God, are prayed for by the Christian community when illness strikes.

Whenever I pray for someone who is physically ill, I always seek to see them as a whole person, as a unity. They do not have a sick body. He or she is a sick person. And since disease and disharmony are results of the Fall, everyone at one time or another suffers from both. In this chapter I will share some of the findings I have made in the last four or five years about prayer for certain illnesses.

Heart Disease

Let me first of all take heart disease. My body has spoken so loudly at times that I have had to listen. One of these times was when I developed coronary heart disease. Fortunately, I am learning to hear what my body is saying, and through the prayers of many people, three heart attacks, and two open-heart surgeries, I am now in good health and hope to live to a ripe old age. I have learned that nobody "catches" coronary heart disease. Nor is inheritance the only cause of it. The problem is psychogenic, as well as hereditary and dietary. It has its beginnings deep within what we call "Junior," or the deep mind, and in the person's reactions to stress.

Stress is not necessarily a bad word or a bad thing, as Dr. Hans Selye, the popularizer of the word, has pointed out. Stress is a God-given gift. In emergencies, it is certainly a good thing. We are so constructed by God that danger causes tremendous physical reactions, like accelerated heartbeat, increased adrenalin flow, and dilated blood vessels. We get ready to fight or run from our would-be assailant, and our bodies are given a new burst of energy.

But if stress becomes dis-stress, it can easily result in dis-ease. Distress is stress that is prolonged with no end or escape in sight. An unpleasant job, where the problems cannot be remedied but which you cannot leave for financial reasons, could lead to distress. Your body responds to the pressure as a threat, but you can neither fight nor flee. Type A people (to use a label created by Dr. Meyer Friedman and Dr. Ray Rosenman) like myself, who want to always stay on top of things, who hurry through meals, work, play, and everything else, who get disgusted with people who don't hurry, and who have some free-floating anger which gets directed at poor drivers, bad umpires, and other aggravations, are particularly prone to distress, and hence to developing coronary heart disease. A particular genetic make-up, which provides the physical setting for heart disease, together with the distress, can cause the problem. The energy-yielding fat pouring into our bloodstreams is slow to metabolize when not used in "fight or flight," lodges in our coronary arteries as plaque, and eventually clogs them. We have all the energy at hand that we need to handle life's situations, but we can't for some reason or another use it constructively, and end up wounded.

Whenever I pray for someone with coronary heart problems, I spend considerable time listening, and am especially aware of any signs of distress, whether in marriage, work, or whatever. To deal with the distress, it is important to hear what the body of the person is saying. Is it telling them to slow down, is it speaking about fear or anger or especially guilt?

The first thing I do is pray for the heart itself. I place one hand over the heart and one hand on the back in the same place. I usually visualize the heart surrounded in light like the pictures of the Sacred Heart of Jesus one sees in some Roman Catholic homes. I then visualize Jesus himself, who is present in the room as the risen Christ through the power of the Spirit, reaching his hands right into the person's chest and holding the heart in his hands. I see his thumbs—in my imagination, of course—gently touching each of the arteries to the heart. I see the cheese-like matter dissolving from inside the arteries, or I see the collateral flow beginning. (Collateral flow takes place when a plugged-off artery routes blood into spare canals provided by God at birth for all of us in case of such an occasion.) In my imagination I see each artery happily relaxed, and I see the blood flowing evenly to the whole body. I often bless the heart, because of all the blood it has so freely pumped over the years. As I have said many times, when people say "Bless your heart" to me, I take it very literally. Incidentally, in that connection I would bless any part of the body which is diseased, just to encourage the organ to perform its proper function happily.

I often speak peace to the heart, using the words of Jesus in John's gospel, "Peace I leave with you; my peace I give to you; not as the world gives do I give to you. Let not your hearts be troubled, neither let them be afraid" (John 14:27 RSV). While I know that Jesus was talking to the whole person in his use of the word "heart," I think that the physical heart of a person is probably the organ most sensitive to the peace of God as well as to distress.

A case history comes to mind, that of a Midwest farmer who asked me to pray for him. I did pray for him, in the basement of the church, with two of his friends present. He was suffering from heart failure. He had *arrhythmia,* or irregular heartbeat, and he had an enlarged heart. The year before he had been to a famous clinic where they had decided they would replace the malfunctioning valves in his heart one month after the time he asked me to pray for him. I put my hand on his heart and prayed, while his friends watched. I visualized the heart shrinking to its normal size, about the size of his fist. I also visualized the valves working perfectly, with no blood washing back when it was not supposed to. And I visualized the pressure and worry and concern he had been having relaxed, so that his whole system could be at peace with the peace of God. I referred to all of this out loud in the prayer. As I prayed for him I remembered that his father had died years before, unexpectedly, of a heart attack. Conscious that there might be fear connected with the same thing happening to him, through prayer I cut off any remaining negative feelings about his father and his death.

When I was through, I thanked the Lord that he had in fact touched his heart. About a month later I received a phone call from a friend of his who had been called from the clinic where they were to do the heart surgery. The surgeons had come in the day before the heart surgery and said that they had decided not to do the surgery because his heart was apparently normal in size, there was no longer any arrhythmia that they could tell, and that if they were to put in new valves, they couldn't put in better ones than he already had, so he could go back home. That is a somewhat atypical case of praying for the heart, but it helped me learn a great deal about hearts and about how the physical heart expresses so much of the person.

Hypertension

Closely related to heart disease is hypertension, or high blood pressure, which is a very common problem from which one out of every five Americans suffers. It can result in strokes and heart disease and kidney failure. One of the biggest factors causing high blood pressure is the use of too much salt. Americans eat four times as much salt as they should, according to one expert. There are a number of effective treatments for hypertension, including drug therapy, behavior changes, weight loss, and reduction in salt intake. I have learned that prayer is very effective in the treatment of hypertension. I pray for relaxation, for painless weight loss and salt reduction and behavioral changes, as it may apply to the particular individual. We urge continuation on medication, no matter how well the individual feels, until the doctor says he can terminate it. It is my experience that people suffering from hypertension are some of the very best candidates for prayer for healing. The hypertension is a symptom which is pointing to a change needed in the life of the person.

Cancer

Many people want to know how to pray for cancer. No one knows the cause of cancer but God. Of course, it is a result of the human Fall, and is one of the major physical diseases that is being battled today. I personally believe some victims of cancer may have an unconscious desire to die, and until they recognize it they may not become well no matter how much I pray. I have prayed for many people with cancer, and many of them have gone into remission. But I do not count a remission the same as a healing, so I encourage people not to discuss any kind of healing for at least two years. In fact, I am very strong about encouraging people to listen to their oncologist as he or she monitors the disease. Together with surgery, chemotherapy, or radiation therapy, we can bring prayer therapy to bear upon the illness and can enhance the whole healing process. Whenever a person with cancer comes to see me, I am most interested in knowing a number of things about their life. I am interested especially in the time up to two years before the onset of the cancer.

What I do in the prayer process with cancer is seek to enlist the body's immune system to fight off the illness. The problem with cancer is the growth of abnormal cells. If it can be enlisted, the body is equipped to fight off the illness. I think that both environment and heredity have something to do with the cause of cancer. I also believe that a deep sorrow, unforgiveness, deep hurt, or loneliness can be among the reasons that "Junior" begins to give up on the whole business of living.

If an immune system does not want to work properly, then cells can grow without being fought against. I realize that there is a tremendous danger of oversimplifying, but it seems to me from all my experience in discussing cancer with oncologists, reading about it, and praying for many people, that the future of cancer destruction lies in immunology.

Having heard the cancer victim's life history, especially concerning the time preceding the onset of the illness, I am ready to pray for the person. When I pray, I speak to the deep mind in the name of Jesus Christ, and speak to every single cell in the body, since probably every cell is a hologram, or three-dimensional picture in miniature, of the entire body. I always remind every cell that Jesus Christ is Lord. And since I know that God created the immune system to fight off illness, it is not hard to pray with faith that the system will do what God intended it to do. As I pray, I visualize the white cells attacking and destroying every abnormal cell in the body. I pray for an increase of the light and energy of God's life. I visualize tumors shrinking.

I will pray repeatedly for people with cancer until the cancer goes into remission. I'm sure there are many things taking place in the prayer process, including acceptance and love by the pray-er, suggestions going into the deep mind, and encouragement of the body's own resources. I'm sure that the use of imagination has a tremendous effect on the destruction of the cancer. I believe that the actual fact of enlisting someone to pray and asking God to heal causes a desire on the part of the person prayed for to get well. As a result, their faith enlarges, along with the possibility of their getting well. But in the end, no matter what message we use, it is God who heals the disease. It is God who heals the disease whether it is by radiation therapy or chemotherapy or surgery or prayer. But I believe that the answer we now have to the war on cancer is prayer.

We often do soaking prayer, for a number of hours at a time, for people who have cancer. We visualize the healing at length. But sometimes when a person has cancer, it is necessary to prepare them for death, because there is a sense in which death is complete healing. On two occasions that I recall, I knew inside myself that it was necessary to prepare the person for death. If a person wants to die, it is almost impossible to pray for them to be healed, because their body is absolutely conforming to their will. That is one reason why mates often die so near in time to each other; when one is gone, the other loses heart and wants to die. But most of the time the ill person can be given at least a few more years through prayer.

Some time ago I prayed for a woman who had so much cancer in her abdomen that she looked nine months pregnant. Months after the prayer I went out to my waiting room to bring someone into my office for prayer, and a woman who was there with the ill person greeted me. Not believing that I had ever met her before, I asked "Do I know you?" It turned out that this was the woman I had prayed for, now looking slim and healthy. She was feeling fine, her doctor was amazed with her progress, and both she and her husband were thrilled that she could now wear a size 9 dress again!

Allergies

I have prayed for many people with allergies, and I have seen a number of cases where allergies have been greatly improved and some altogether healed. It is difficult to know how to pray for allergies, because I feel they are directly related to the make-up of the whole person. But it is not hard to pray against allergies with faith, because I do not think that God intends us to be at disharmony with the created order. I do not think that God intends us to be allergic to certain good foods and especially to animals and plants. Therefore I come to someone with an allergy with a confident knowledge that the allergy is saying something about the individual. As a matter of fact, one of the questions we ask in almost every illness is, "What is the illness saying to you?" And in an allergic situation the allergy is often saying something like, "The peace of God needs to come to this person. They need to relax and roll with the punches of life. There is no need to become tense." And with that in mind, I listen to the whole case history and begin to pray.

When we pray for allergies, we are most intent on praying for the peace of God to come, for harmony with the created order. I can't understand why one should continue to be allergic to dogs and cats, for example, when they are created for our enjoyment. In the case of allergies, I pray for the glandular system, that there will be a perfect balance of hormones and glandular secretions throughout the whole body, that whatever is reacting to the particular allergen will accept it and that the message will get through to the deep mind that there no longer needs to be a battle over it.

I know that certain allergies can be used advantageously in life, and that some people never get rid of them because they can have benefits. For example, why should I peel potatoes when I am allergic to them, and someone else can do it for me? Or, why should I take care of the dog if I'm allergic to her and somebody else can do the job? Once the allergy starts, it may easily be maintained, even without the person being conscious of it, because it makes life easier. I believe there is a chemical reason for allergies, which is probably genetic, but which because of the environment has become one of the weak links in the body's reactions. I would encourage all people with allergies to go to an allergist to receive shots to build up immunity, and when I pray I pray in conjunction with the medication and with the therapy being offered by the doctor. In fact, I might even want to talk to the doctor about the allergy and seek to understand exactly what's causing it.

A pastor I've known for many years was allergic to citrus fruits and asked to be prayed for about it at a seminar. After he had returned home, he wrote me later, he dreamed that he was being chased by a tiger. But instead of letting the tiger keep chasing him, he turned around and faced it. He wrote that when he awoke, he went right to the kitchen and drank a big glass of orange juice, with no ill effects. He knew that in this dream his unconscious mind was trying to tell him something about himself and his relation to his environment, and he was sensitive enough to listen and understand.

Obesity

There are many people in our society who are suffering from obesity, or overweight. Most Americans gain about a pound a year during their adult life, so by the time they are 50 they are 25 or more pounds overweight. Most of us would be better off if we kept to the weight that we were at age 25. Other people struggle with their weight from childhood, and many never conquer the problem. Overweight is dangerous because the heart must pump blood through all that extra tissue, and the size of the circulatory system must increase with each pound of weight that is added, making the heart's job that much more difficult. There are also cosmetic reasons for avoiding overweight, and often excess weight becomes a serious emotional as well as physical problem. People who are lonely often gain weight trying to satisfy their emotional hunger by eating.

Many people desire to get rid of the weight but seem not to be able to. The best way to get rid of weight is to cut down on one's eating. There is no substitute for that; and it should be done slowly and steadily, on a long-range basis.

When I pray for people who are overweight, I pray about the reasons why they're overeating. Is the eating a substitute for love? Is it to satisfy loneliness? Is the person bored? Are they in a situation where eating has just become a habit? Many people seem to starve themselves all day, but then sit in front of the television and eat all evening. When I pray for a person, I want to be careful in articulating some of the above things. Prayer will not work any magic or make the pounds just drop off by themselves. But it can help eliminate some of the causes of the overeating, and help the person develop willpower.

It is also important to develop the overweight person's self-image, to help them to learn not to think of themselves as fat. When I pray for them, I visualize the fat running off their bodies, and I see them in a new suit or dress standing in front of a mirror, proud that they have lost weight.

I would use the same approach, in fact, for any "addiction," whether it's addiction to food, cigarettes, or drugs. The reason for the problem can be removed through prayer, and the person can learn to affirm being without the problem. Of course, if there is a metabolic problem, and they are few and far between, prayer can also be of help in adjusting the body's processes.

Anorexia Nervosa

It is an equally serious problem when weight loss becomes excessive, to the point of *anorexia nervosa,* which I have prayed for on a number of occasions. This complete loss of appetite usually strikes perfectionistic, intense young women who diet until they are unable to stop. It can be turned around if one understands the personality complex out of which this illness arises. The young woman needs to regain her will to live, to allow her body to follow its instincts for survival. She needs to adjust her self-image, which may be distorted, just as the overweight person does. She needs to know that it is not God's will that we starve ourselves to death, only that we eat in moderation; she needs God's acceptance and love. As with the person who is overweight, I would have the person suffering from anorexia nervosa affirm an ideal weight, repeating many times a day, "I enjoy weighing ____ pounds, and I will live to a ripe old age."

Back Problems

Back problems have increased in occurrence in our day. Back pain has become as much an expression of tension as the common headache. Through prayer, we can deal with the tensions at the root of the problem, as well as the possible physical and anatomical problems, and the pain can be relieved.

My wife, Marcine, is a most striking example of what prayer can do for back problems. She has had back problems off and on for many years. Sometimes the pain has become almost unbearable for her. She has seen a number of orthopedic surgeons, all of whom have given her medication and recommended absolute bed rest. Several years ago she was having one of these episodes of extreme back pain. It was so bad that she couldn't even stand up straight.

She had been in bed for a couple of days when I prayed for her with the laying-on of hands one night when I came to bed. I asked God to heal her completely, although it was clear from the way she hobbled to the bathroom she was in a bad way. Then we went to sleep.

I was awakened in the middle of the night by Marcine telling me that there was someone in the room, and they were holding on to her feet. I sat up and looked around. Seeing no one, I lay back down again, telling her she was dreaming. Again she said "Bill!" in that tone she uses when she really wants me to listen. I looked over at her, and she was lying stiff as a board in bed. She insisted that someone was holding on to her feet, and she was just petrified. I looked again and could still not see anyone. We finally laughed, but then we were filled with awe as we realized that it might have been an angel. In a few minutes the "angel-vise" stopped. Marcine got up and walked to the bathroom, perfectly well.

Scoliosis is a serious back problem, a curvature of the spine which occurs usually in young people during times of rapid growth—the vertebrae grow faster on one side than the other.

This problem can be prayed for, and I urge you to see *I Prayed, He Answered* for the story of our family's experience. In prayer for scoliosis I have actually felt the spine of people move ever so gradually. People suffering from scoliosis should use the cast or whatever the doctor recommends in addition to the praying, although I believe that prayer can sometimes make the surgery or cast unnecessary. When I pray for scoliosis, I pray for a straight spine and that the sides of the spine will grow in perfect accordance with the will of God for the individual. I also urge people not to think of themselves as having scoliosis, but to visualize themselves having a perfectly straight spine, and to affirm a straight spine several times daily, so the deep mind hears what it is supposed to do. I have found that the deep mind is a willing servant who will do whatever we tell it to do. If I can learn to consciously communicate with that deep mind, as I am doing every day unconsciously by the conversation I am carrying on with myself all the time, then I can enable my body to come more into perfect harmony with God's will.

Lupus

Systemic lupus erythematosus is an inflammatory disease of the connective tissue of unknown origin, occurring predominantly in women. It is often a very serious illness. The first time I prayed for someone with lupus I used a soaking prayer. I was visiting a congregation, and the pastor told me there was a woman in the church who had lupus, who had suffered greatly and for whom there was no apparent cure. The pastor asked if I would be willing to pray for her. I agreed to do so with the request that three or four others would pray with me, and that we would pray for her throughout the whole afternoon.

We gathered together and made sure that she was lying down comfortably; then the three or four of us who were present worshiped the Lord privately and with song and short prayers. After becoming aware of the Lord's presence, and becoming convinced that our Lord loved the woman and wanted to touch her, we began to pray for her, taking turns as God seemed to lay it on our hearts.

In the course of my prayer, I saw the woman in my mind's eye like an anatomical model made of clear plastic. In my imagination I saw this plastic model of the woman filled with all kinds of greasy, dirty substances, symbolizing in my mind the poison or whatever it was in her system which was not gotten rid of by her immune system. She was subject to infections constantly because this system did not work properly. As I was praying I thought to visualize plugs in her fingers and her toes, and to see those plugs being pulled and all the poison draining out. As I prayed, I saw all the poison draining out of her arms and her feet until she was empty inside. The traces of poison were still on the inside of the plastic, like a dirty glass which had held some juice. Then it occurred to me to visualize the top of her head with a lid on it, and I asked the Lord to send two of his holy angels with a hose and a heavenly detergent, to open up the top of her head and to squirt this detergent in until the whole model became perfectly clear, like a shining glass just out of the dishwasher. Then I visualized the plugs in her fingers and toes being placed back in.

I asked the Lord to send those two angels with a kind of liquid love, to fill her up with this, and that her body would respond to it. So after seeing the plugs put in in my imagination, I began to see her filled from the toes up to the calves and knees, up to the waist and chest and shoulders, neck and head, absolutely perfectly filled with the love of Jesus Christ. Then we closed the top of her head, and we thanked the Lord that he had done a really thorough job of cleansing her.

After praying for three or four hours, we discontinued prayer, and I left that particular town. Some time later I was speaking in a church not far from the town where I'd prayed for the woman with lupus, and I was telling the story of how this picture had come to me. In the midst of my discussion of the imagery I had used, a woman stood up and said, "I wonder, Pastor, if I could finish the story."

Not recognizing her, I said, "Who are you?"

She said, "I am the woman you prayed for." She stood up and told the crowd gathered there that two or three days following the prayer she had gotten blisters under her toenails and under her fingernails, and that in the course of the weeks and months since then her disease had gone into remission, and she was apparently completely and perfectly healed of lupus. I have not seen the lady for a year or two so I do not know what the results have been, but I hope that she has continued her progress toward physical, as well as emotional and spiritual, health.

Epilepsy

Epilepsy is a disease which evidences itself in seizures. In these seizures, consciousness may be lost, or there may be just a small amount of involuntary movement or twitching. Most epileptic conditions can be controlled through medication. We can be grateful that this is so, and I urge people to continue their medication.

However, there are times when it appears as though the medication does not work. Recently I had a case of a little three-year-old who was having many epileptic seizures every night. His father had not slept apart from him for six months. The boy had been treated in hospitals by all kinds of physicians. He had even been taken to an exorcist, his parents fearing that there was some demonic infiltration.

They came to me as a kind of last resort, and as I listened to the whole story and looked at the little boy sleeping, it came to me that I should pray for the parents, for specific guidance for them as to what their move should be. So after listening to them for an hour or so I went behind them and put my hands on the parents, with the mother holding the child, and prayed for guidance. Here were parents who were at the end of their tether, and I asked God to give them guidance within the next few days, if possible, that they would know what to do with their child.

In the next few days following the prayer, they were led to take the child to a chiropractor, and, after one or two manipulations, the child ceased to have any seizures whatsoever, and has been fine ever since. The chiropractor became a vehicle for God's healing. I have prayed for a number of epileptics who have claimed complete healing after six months or a year's time. Whether they are healed or not, I couldn't say. All I know is that I have prayed for them, and they have felt better.

Headaches

Approximately 20,000,000 Americans suffer from headaches bad enough to make them seek medical help. In fact, it is the most common of all problems that are brought to physicians. Headaches are difficult to sort out, because they come in different varieties, and the current medical wisdom on the topic leaves one bewildered by the complexities and confusion and missing links in our knowledge.

Tension headaches are the easiest to pray for, I have found. It is difficult for an individual to pray for himself with regard to many illnesses, and especially headaches, because when you go to pray about headaches, you usually think "headache," and the tension increases. Only after learning meditation and relaxation techniques was I able to overcome tension headaches myself.

The most difficult type of headache is the migraine, which comes from the Greek word meaning "half the skull," a reasonable designation since this type of headache is often confined to one side of the head. The underlying bond for all headaches labeled "migraine" is the role played by the blood vessels of the neck and head. There is evidence that the symptoms are usually related to the constriction of these vessels and that the actual headache occurs when the vessels subsequently expand. The exact reasons for these changes in the blood vessels are not certain. It's important in the treatment of these and other headaches to determine the factor or factors which trigger them, which may be dietary or hormonal or emotional. They are usually treated through careful drug therapy, with aspirin, codeine and the like.

It has been my experience that migraine headaches are often the turning of one's anger back on one's own head. In other words, it is very possible that your own head is "taking the rap" for whatever is going on in the way of stress. Biofeedback is being used for people who have the emotional factors that cause some headaches. Meditation, particularly Christian meditation, can be extremely effective in battling headaches. Just repeating the name "Jesus" can have a demonstrably soothing effect on the mind and body. I have prayed for many people over the years who have been completely relieved of headaches, including migraines. Removing the source of stress, or learning to cope with it, is the key.

Multiple Sclerosis

I have never seen a person with multiple sclerosis healed, but I have seen many of them go into remission; whether the remission was spontaneous or caused by the prayer, I do not know. It is my impression of them as people that the amount of current traveling over the wires, the nerves, to the various parts of the body is too strong or has too much voltage, and that this knocks the insulation off the nerves. If it is possible to pray for peace and rest to come to the individual, so that he or she can slow down and be at peace emotionally, a complete change might be brought about. When the sheath has been knocked off the nerves, it is very difficult to pray about because the sheath is not something that the body is able to replace. We do not have the physical capability to rebuild the nerve insulation through prayer, but the change in emotional behavior brought about through prayer can send the illness into remission and lessen the severity of the symptoms.

Diabetes

I have prayed for many people suffering from diabetes, and I have seen some evidence of remission in the case of younger children. For those who have been diabetics for a number of years I have not seen any major changes. I have talked to people who have been healed of diabetes by prayer, but I myself have not seen an adult healed. I have seen children whose pancreas began producing more insulin as a result of prayer both on my part and by the parents, but one must be extremely cautious not to raise exaggerated hopes. With diabetes, as with other serious illnesses, the person must keep taking the prescribed medication or therapy until his regular doctor recommends its discontinuation.

Arthritis

Arthritis is a common problem which causes many people a great deal of pain. There are over 100 causes of arthritis (literal definition: "inflammation of a joint"), many of which are completely curable. Rheumatoid arthritis, which affects about five million people in this country, has an unknown cause. The treatment of rheumatoid arthritis usually follows four courses: rest, physical therapy, drugs, and surgery. Aspirin is still the best drug treatment. Osteoarthritis (about 10 million in the country) is due to mechanical "wear and tear." Most elderly people have signs of joint degeneration, but few, comparatively, suffer from it. Whenever I pray for someone who has arthritis, I am interested in finding out why the immune system of the body seems to be overworking. While people who have cancer have immune systems that are underworking, the opposite may be true with arthritis. In fact, I have learned to be careful not to pray that the immune system will slow down too drastically, but rather that it will become "just right." People with rheumatoid arthritis often find it difficult to reveal their deepest feelings. They may find it difficult, because of fear of rejection, to say "no" when they mean "no," and "yes" when they mean "yes." I ask an arthritic to paint a picture in words of their life in about 20 minutes, using large brushstrokes. I listen for anger, rejection, guilt, hostility, and so on, praying, of course, while I am listening.

I then pray that the immune system, which is working so hard that it is apparently building extra cells into the joints, will just slow down and be at peace. I ask that the child in the person will be able to come forth, that the shining, bright, real person might be seen and that the person will see themselves through Christ's eyes. Arthritis is hard to pray for, but it will yield to prayer. I don't expect it to go away immediately (though I'm not surprised if it does), but rather think of the prayer as a seed which is planted, but which needs time to grow. To quote an old truism, an arthritic needs to "let go and let God" (so do we all!).

Several years ago a woman attended one of my missions who was so badly crippled with rheumatoid arthritis that she could hardly do her own housework. She was in much pain and had difficulty getting around. The night she attended was the night we do healing of the memories. Following my discussion I led the audience in an actual prayer in which I asked Christ to walk back through our lives, healing our memories. During the prayer this woman and her husband heard me say, "There is someone here in pain." They have gone over the tape of the session many times since then and cannot find any place where I said such a thing. But that's what both of them heard. When they heard me say this, this woman began feeling a sensation of heat, starting from the tips of her toes and going all the way up through her body. She was absolutely healed sitting right in her pew, and has been fine ever since. She and her husband have since been active in supporting and participating in our ministry, so I see her from time to time.

With arthritis, as with all prayer for healing, I would try to get from the person an acceptance of healing. It is important that the person not affirm the problem, thereby accepting its existence. If you say, "I have [or I'm going to get] arthritis" long enough, you will probably get it. Both the pray-er and the prayee should learn to reject doubt. When you pray for someone the second or third time, come to the prayer with complete faith, no matter what the outward signs are, and look for the growth of the seed of healing which was planted in the first prayer. It will grow, but not if you keep pulling up the seed to check on whether it was planted right in the first place.

6

PRAYING FOR MENTAL HEALING

Praying for the mentally ill is more difficult for me than praying about physical distress. I'm not sure why that is, but it is my experience that it's easier to get the body through prayer to harmonize with the purposes of God than it is to get the mind to harmonize with the purposes of God.

At the present time two million Americans are being treated for mental illness. There are many forms of mental illness. The two most common in America today are *schizophrenia* ("a divided mind") and *depression.*

Schizophrenia

Schizophrenia is a mental disorder marked by a progressive withdrawal from reality, grossly inappropriate behavior, and a discrepancy between thought content and mood; that is, the patient may smile while saying that they are about to die. Disturbances of mental function include delusions and hallucinations. Almost everyone who comes to me suffering from schizophrenia is on some type of drug, and many have been hospitalized. Antipsychotic drugs, while they really only mask the symptoms, can help the ill person for a time and make it possible for them to receive therapy. That single fact of drugs is probably what has reduced the number of people in state mental hospitals so much since the mid-1950s.

But the problem of schizophrenia has not lessened. No one really knows its cause. There is some evidence for a genetic predisposition to psychosis. For example, schizophrenia is more likely to occur in both members of an identical twin pair, who have exactly the same genetic composition, than in both members of a fraternal twin pair, who are no more similar than other siblings. Research is being done on the possibility that a chemical or chemicals in the brain might be responsible for the problem.

The onset of schizophrenia can be triggered by an event with a critical personal meaning for the person. It could be a loss, especially of a person to whom the patient has been close. When a susceptible person is faced with an acute loss, he or she may choose one of three alternatives for dealing with the unbearable pain: homicide, suicide, or psychosis. In schizophrenia the patient chooses psychosis and withdraws from a reality they can't endure any longer. Illness, then, is the option the individual takes to survive, given their genetic background, early developmental history, and their current environment of pain and frustration. This compromise between the patient's unbearable pain and the related rage, and the need to survive, contains an element of choice that is crucial to understanding the development of the psychosis-vulnerable individual.

When a schizophrenic person comes to see me, whether I spend much time listening or just get right at the praying depends on how ill they are. If the person is suffering extremely, the most important thing I can do is love them and care for them and realize we have more in common than separates us, and that I am a messenger, a representative of God's love. If the person is in drug therapy and seems as if they want to discuss their situation, I may spend time listening, but my chief concern is not to give counsel or advice, but to listen and to pray.

When I pray for a schizophrenic, I usually pray for and about the fear which he or she is experiencing and the anxiety that goes along with it. Since God has not given us a spirit of fear, but of "strength, love, and self-discipline" (2 Tim. 1:7), and since "perfect love banishes fear" (1 John 4:18), then I need to come out boldly against that fear and speak to it as to a darkness, telling it to leave the individual, and asking for the person's mind and heart to be filled with the love of Christ.

In one sense, this is like an exorcism, but in another it is completely different from it. Generally speaking, the mentally ill are not demon-possessed, but may be troubled by an internal spirit of fear, which needs to be treated most gently with a person who is ill. The last thing a person needs to hear when they are mentally ill is that they have been infiltrated by the devil.

So after speaking to the fear, and believing the promise that perfect love banishes fear, and remembering that the best picture of perfect love is the cross of Jesus, and that the cross has the power to cast fear out, then in my imagination I see the fear going out, and I believe the promise. I discipline my mind to reject the idea that the fear has not gone. I accept the healing for the person, much as I would accept forgiveness or salvation or any other gift of God. Then I go about praying for the healing of the memories of the individual.

In praying for the healing of memories I will probably go back even to the time before the foundations of the world were laid, when God thought about making this individual and chose how this person would come into being. I pray about the coming together of a certain set of parents, and the conception of the child. At the conception of the person I visualize Christ as the healing light of God present; I visualize

Christ being present in his healing light and power all through the gestation period. I visualize Christ there all the way up until the child is born, and during the birth process, and following the trauma of birth, and through everything that took place after that all the way through the person's life.

I keep myself open to any guidance or leading that may come, or any pictures that may come to me that will cause me to pray according to the special will of God for that individual. Sometimes a picture will come to mind of something in the person's life about which I have never been told, but which it turns out is precisely what happened. I am not surprised if I am given a sense of what is going on with the schizophrenic.

I know that when I've prayed the seed is planted, though I realize that the patient probably doesn't have any faith about it, so I don't lay any burden on them. In fact, I tell the person to let me worry about it, to go away and come back in a week to ten days. It may take three months of praying for a person, time after time, to get them out of the illness. They will also need to be called on from time to time to make sure that what has happened because of the prayers has stabilized. And since we have learned that most healing is progressive or processive, we are willing to pray and to watch until healing comes. While God could heal directly, in a moment of time, generally that is not the way he does it, but he enlists the faith of his church to stand by and remain with and be consistent and caring about those who are ill.

I will never forget praying after one of my missions for a young boy suffering from schizophrenia. During the course of the prayer, I addressed the fear in him directly, as I often do, saying, "In Jesus' name, I command you to leave!"

Immediately the boy jumped up and said, "It left!" He was much improved after the prayer, as are many schizophrenics who are prayed for. It is a tough problem to lick, but prayer can help a great deal, and occasionally schizophrenics are perfectly healed.

Depression

Depression is a word used to identify normal reactions to the sorrows of life, as well as serious mood disturbances. In one sense depression may be called the common cold of mental illness, because there are more people suffering from depression than from any other kind of mental illness. Classic and full-blown depression is usually described in terms of the loss of the capacity to enjoy life, combined with a poverty of thought and movement. The symptoms might include weight loss, decreased sexual desire, difficulty in sleeping, and fatigue. Serious depression may sometimes be expressed in agitation or excessive complaints about body function or chronic pain, especially headaches. There are some diseases that can cause depression, like hypothyroidism, heart disease, and arthritis. There are even certain drugs which can cause depression, particularly steroids. Since the range of manifestation of depression is almost endless, there is no easy rule of thumb for recognizing it, except the observation that if it interferes with a person's ability to function in basic ways, in eating or sleeping or working or relating to other people, then professional help should be sought.

Fortunately, most people with severe depression can be helped, and what psychiatrists do most of the time is to first reduce the symptoms and, in serious cases, to prevent thoughts and intentions of suicide. Suicide is a common and tragic result of serious depression, and conservative estimates put suicide attempts at over a quarter of a million per year in the United States, with about 25,000 of them ending in death. In fact, it is the second leading cause of death in the 15-to-24 age group. So one of the ways in which depression is attacked immediately by psychiatrists is to decrease the possibility of suicide by the desperate person. Antidepressive drugs are most commonly used for this today. Of course, these drugs should be administered under the supervision of a physician, because they have side effects, such as low blood pressure or heart rhythm abnormalities. These drugs should especially be used with caution in people with certain forms of heart disease, including heart attacks.

Another drug which has been most helpful in one form of depression is lithium carbonate, which has been used since 1949 for controlling a variant of depressive disease known as *manic-depression.* In manic-depressive disease there are swings of mood from depression to episodes of mania, or exaggerated activity and overexcitement. Lithium is effective in preventing attacks of mania, and, to a lesser degree, depression. Lithium may require several weeks to exert its effect and must be carefully monitored with routine blood tests.

Manic-depressive disease often has no obvious cause. Much more common are mood changes which are provoked by external events, such as the death of a loved one, marital discord, or serious illness. Grieving is a normal response to a loss, and the failure to grieve may lead to psychosomatic symptoms months or even years later. If grief reactions continue beyond several months, however, or if they interfere seriously with the capacity for work, they are cause for concern. Depression is also a common problem among women today, with many women suffering from feelings of lack of self-worth, boredom, and uncertainty about their role in the world.

When a person comes to me who is either depressed or suffering from manic-depression, I first learn whether he has been to a psychiatrist to be treated, perhaps with drugs. While I know the drugs deal mainly with the symptoms, I am interested in getting the person up out of the pits as soon as possible. Then I begin to pray for the person who is feeling down. I do not come to them with the kind of optimism that believes they are going to walk out of my office as high as a kite. I rather believe that it will probably take a number of times of prayer before they will be healed, and that we're going to have to pray for spiritual and emotional and physical healing. Sometimes

I get the feeling the person is physically ill, and that they might need a thyroid check, or might need to go off a certain medication; if that is the case, I will recommend they see a medical doctor. But I often feel when I meet with a person who is in depression that the medications are dealing only with the symptoms and that we need to get at the root cause of the depression. Is the person not having fellowship or good relations with the members of their family? Is the person guilty, and do they need to deal with the guilt? Has there been some event that has triggered the depression? Has there been a severe loss of some kind? There are many other things that I might ask and pray about.

In any case, I focus on the healing of the memories of the person's whole life, concentrating on events within a few months of the depression's onset. I find out about what the person wants from life and why they're being held back. I seek to pray in the direction of asking the light of God's presence to come in and heal that depression. I am very interested in getting the person to discover what the depression is saying, and what it means by what it is saying. Why is it happening, and what would change what's happening? Once those things have become clear, and they often do not become clear in the first or second session, then I can pray with concrete prayers with regard to what needs healing in the person.

Recently a minister came to me with deep depression, the second time he had suffered from this condition. He had gone to two psychiatrists who had put him on antidepressant medication, and although he could exist on those drugs, he knew they weren't dealing with the real problem. We had two or three sessions together, in which I listened to his aspirations and his hurts and other feelings. Then each time I prayed. After a few sessions he came out of his depression, and is now back in the parish feeling happy. He needed rest, he felt guilty about many things, he needed to know that someone cared for him, he needed to be assured by his parish that he was loved—

all these things were part of it. But more than anything, he needed to know the love of Christ. He needed to know that Jesus had not left him, and when that assurance came, joy came to his heart, as joy comes to the heart of the little child who knows he or she is loved.

Neuroses

We are often called on to pray for neuroses, and the common denominator for this range of psychological behavioral responses is anxiety. Neurotic responses are generally less disruptive than psychosis, but some, such as severe phobias or compulsions, can markedly impair both work and social adjustment. There are some neurotic behaviors which are clearly abnormal, such as washing one's hands every five minutes because of a fear of germs. More often neuroses are expressed indirectly, in fatigue or irritability or depression. Complaints about body functions, or actual symptoms such as numbness or heart palpitations, may be an expression of anxiety. And some neurotic behaviors are extensions of common behaviors, like the handwashing compulsion. The complaints connected with neurosis are often so vague that it is difficult to decide what help is needed. It's usually helpful to evaluate the individual's ability to function in basic ways. If the routines of life are impaired by anxiety, then help should be sought.

I have prayed for many people with neurotic behavior patterns. The range of psychotherapeutic and behavioral treatments for neurosis is almost endless. There are some very good kinds of therapy, and there are some which claim success but which might better be avoided. There are anti-anxiety drugs, known as minor tranquilizers, like Valium, which can be used. But I find that the peace of God, the forgiveness of God, the love of God, can do more to heal the neurotic person than any psychotherapy or drug.

At one of my missions I saw a woman who had a neurotic

habit of cracking her bones. She could crack every bone in her body and did so compulsively. It turned out that when she was small she had promised God that she would never crack her bones again in her life. Of course, she hadn't been able to keep the promise, and her haunting guilt and anxiety had driven her to the point where she could not keep the problem from her mind, and so she couldn't stop cracking her bones. All she needed to be told was that God accepted her as she was, bone-cracking and all, and that he was not going to reject her for breaking a promise she made as a little girl. Many compulsive habits can be eliminated if their forbidden aspect is removed; they then lose their power over us. Once we realize God's gracious acceptance of us, anxiety may leave to be replaced by trust in God's love.

Homosexuality

I have prayed for many homosexuals over the last three or four years, and have listened with great pain to their stories. I have sought to be empathetic and sympathetic, and have sought to treat their particular problem as I would treat any other difficult situation. Nearly all the homosexuals I have met are in deep pain, feeling a great deal of loneliness and guilt and anxiety. Years ago I heard Agnes Sanford pray for a homosexual, and I have prayed in the same way, and have seen a number of lives changed because of it.

We can picture the creativity which God gives in our sexuality like a beautiful stream running its course, with good, clear water and a deep river bed. With the homosexual, for some reason there has been a damming up of that creative and procreative power, and the banks are flooded and the stream diverted. The creative power becomes diffused. In prayer for homosexuals I visualize that flooded river and picture that stream going back into its normal, deep channel by the grace of God. I see the person radiantly happy, creative in the best sense of that term, deeply thankful for his or her own normal sexuality, and accepting that gift from God with all its potential.

I view homosexuality as basically a rejection of a gift of God. I think it is probably also a sin, but in no way do I condemn any homosexual, any more than I condemn a gossip or an egotist or a thief. It may take a number of prayers, and it takes a great deal of faith to believe that God's intended gift can be recovered, but it can and should be done. In our society, where there has been so much repression of our sexuality and the expression of sexuality in bizarre and sometimes sick forms, the Christian church should bind itself together in believing prayer, so that the gift of God's creative power can be restored in the lives of all of us.

Alcoholism

When one considers that half of all deaths in automobile accidents and half of all homicides and a fourth of all suicides are related to alcohol abuse, that people with a "drinking problem" are seven times more likely to be separated or divorced than those in the general population, that the total cost of alcohol abuse in this country may exceed 44 billion dollars per year, that an alcoholic's life span is shortened an average of 10 or 12 years, and that at least 10 million persons in this country abuse alcohol, it is no wonder that it is one of the things people ask us to pray for, for themselves or their loved ones. Except for war and hunger, alcoholism is the most devastating sociomedical problem faced by our society today.

If you gathered a group of experts together to define alcoholism, you would have as many definitions as there are experts. The Rutgers University Center of Alcoholic Studies has stated that "an alcoholic is one who is unable consistently to choose whether he shall drink or not, and who, if he drinks, is unable consistently to choose whether he shall stop or not."

Whatever the reasons behind alcoholism, one thing is sure: if an alcoholic does not stop drinking, he or she is going to end up in one of three places: prison, an institution for emotional disorders, or the morgue. The physical effects of excessive drinking include liver damage, gastrointestinal problems, damage to the nervous system, and heart disease. The effects on the drinker's emotional life and the life of his or her family are obvious.

There are many approaches to problem drinking being used today. There is aversion therapy, in which a drug is given so that severe nausea and vomiting occur when the patient drinks alcohol; there is psychotherapy and other psychological approaches; and there are clinics. I have seen more people helped through Alcoholics Anonymous than by any other approach to alcoholism.

The chance for success in the treatment of alcoholism, whether through aversion therapy, psychotherapy, Alcoholics Anonymous, or prayer, is directly proportional to the degree to which a person is willing to acknowledge that he or she is an alcoholic. If a person comes to me admitting they're an alcoholic and desiring to be healed, I am very happy to pray for them. The key to recovery from alcoholism is the willingness to acknowledge the problem, which is really a confession of sin. If there is repentance, God will not only forgive, but will root out that deep thirst in the person and heal them.

I usually start out rather superficially, with prayer that the taste buds of the person will be affected so that they develop an extreme distaste for liquor. I then go deeper into the personality of the person, until I can pray for an absolute yielding up of the problem, a turning away from alcoholism, and a turning to God. Then I pray for a complete cleansing of the whole body and spirit. I follow up with a number of prayers for the person from time to time. I have seen cases where people have walked away from alcohol. Those who have been alcoholics need to stay away from alcohol from then on, because even small amounts can cause the person to lose control again. The person needs to lead a very different life, like a conversion.

After an evening talk at a church, when there were many people waiting to be prayed for, I asked two of our children, who were then in college, to help me. I didn't know what sorts of problems they'd have to pray for, but I needed the help. A woman who was an alcoholic was brought to our daughter Joanna for prayer—not the easiest thing to start with. Joanna prayed about the woman's taste buds and for the healing of her body and spirit, as she had heard me do. We learned one year later that the woman had been completely healed of alcoholism—through the prayer of a novice. This points up our role as a channel for healing in prayer—the healing originates with God, not with us.

Prayer for Children

Praying for children who are disturbed sometimes requires a different approach than you would use for adults. I have found visualization to be exceedingly helpful.

Some little children have definite physical and emotional problems; others may simply be looking for attention. Once my wife told me about a disruptive little boy in her Bible school class. He had been brought in from the nearby community. His parents were not members of the church. After two or three days my wife was exhausted with trying to quiet the boy and get his attention. She finally asked if I would see him. I brought him into my office at the church. He was really a cute little boy, blonde with blue eyes. He looked at me as if I was probably going to beat him up when he came into my office. We had a picture there of Jesus hanging on the cross, and I could imagine him saying to himself, "That's what happens to people when they come in this office."

It wasn't long before I had the little boy on my lap. I asked him if he had ever played baseball. He said he had, so I asked, "Have you ever hit a home run?"

He said, "No, but I've got on base."

I said, "Could you picture yourself hitting a home run?" So we closed our eyes and we imagined him hitting a home run, and rounding first and second. We watched the ball go way over the left-fielder's head, and then saw him pass third, and then we visualized his teammates all standing up as he came into home base, shaking his hand and telling him how great he was. As we talked, I could actually feel the boy smile. Then I asked the Lord that the little boy would see that's the way people really felt about him, that the little trouble within him would be healed, that he wouldn't need to disrupt the class, and that he wouldn't need to cause problems, because the teacher loved him and the kids loved him, just as he was.

After just one prayer the boy was completely transformed. In fact, his mother called the Bible school to ask what we had done with the child, because he was like a different boy. Jesus Christ had touched him.

Children who are adopted often need special prayers and visualization. The Russians, in an experiment, separated a mother rabbit from her babies and took the mother rabbit to the bottom of the sea, a thousand miles away from the babies. They put biofeedback sensors on the mother, and then killed the babies. There was a reaction on the part of the mother, a thousand miles away, at exactly the moment the babies were killed. If that relationship exists in the animal world, how much more so in the human world. A child who has lost his or her mother, through rejection or death, often suffers deep wounds that need to be healed, no matter how happy they are in their adoptive family.

If a child is brought up in a home by adoptive parents who are very understanding, it is a blessing, of course. But often the weight of any problems the child has begins to be focused on the adoption. So what we do is pray for the healing of the memories of that child, going way back to his or her conception, through the birth process, through the separation from the natural mother, which is perceived as rejection by the infant. A child just a week old can already distinguish its mother's voice from other voices, and if that mother's voice is taken away and a new person takes the child, there is hurt. So we ask Jesus to heal that hurt, and he does.

Children are extremely receptive to prayer. Perhaps if we all were prayed for from childhood, we would grow to be more healthy, happy adults. Now that we are learning about prayer, this is a possibility for our children and grandchildren; and if, in prayer, we become like children, then it may be a possibility for us, as well.

7

PRAYING FOR SPECIAL NEEDS

Prayer has far-reaching implications for our lives, beyond prayers for healing. I think that it is true that we are carrying on a conversation with ourselves 90% of the time, and that we become what we say to ourselves. "As a man thinks, so is he," says Proverbs. William James said that any idea held constantly before the mind must come into reality. Whatever we visualize and hold before our minds becomes a reality, whether it is good or bad. Job realized this when he said that the thing he had feared most had come upon him (Job 3:25). Insofar as our thoughts are prayers—for they often are as powerful as prayers—we are in a kind of constant prayer; and we should aim to shape those thoughts to make them fit as prayers. The Bible urges us often to think of things that are above, not of things that are lowly.

Praying with Visualization

Everything in our lives is a matter for thought; everything in our lives is a matter for prayer. We need to learn to use visualizing, which we do naturally when we think, in prayer as well. We can lift our thoughts, even about the routine and ordinary, into our prayers. God has so arranged the nature of things that we know reality by faith. When we have sight, we don't need faith. But in this world we do not have sight, and some day we may discover that the reality which we see around us is only the scratchings of little children who are just beginning to draw.

I have learned to pray about almost everything with the use of visualization to increase faith. God has given us the power to make a picture; and that picture means believing that it shall be so. To the God who has his eye on every sparrow and who numbers the hairs on your head, nothing is too small to be brought up in prayer.

Some years ago, during the time in which Philip was being prayed for by Agnes Sanford, he had a recurring sleeping dream in which he saw himself, Agnes, his cousin, a friend of ours, and me, standing by a building. He got the seuse in this dream that the building was a school or institute, having to do with prayer. Soon Philip, his cousin, and I were having excited discussions on our back patio about this dream, which we came to speak of as the Life Institute. While we "knew" it was an impossibility, we couldn't help dreaming and talking about it, even drawing up plans. In the meantime, my own ministry of teaching and prayer was developing, and became Preaching and Prayer Ministries.

Now the Life Institute exists. Through a series of amazing "coincidences," it has found a home in a beautiful facility in Issaquah, near Seattle, Washington. The Life Institute is a home base for Preaching and Prayer Ministries and the teaching missions I conduct across the country. It is above all else a house of prayer—a place where people can come to be prayed for and loved, to learn how to pray effectively for others, or to be refreshed spiritually. The dream became a reality. The thing we held before our minds—hardly thinking it possible, but all the while seeking God's will in it—came into being, against all appearances, by God's gracious action.

While we were dreaming about the Life Institute, we were hardly aware that our dreaming could help make it a reality. But you can train your power of "dreaming," or visualization, and channel that power into your prayer concerns. For example, suppose that someone in your family is not a Christian. The first thing that is necessary to be of any help to that person is to know God's will, whether God wants them to be a Christian. The Scriptures say that God desires all people to be saved and come to the knowledge of the truth. So it is God's will that your relative become a Christian. Now, we can go to God and ask that that person will become a Christian, saying, "If it be your will," as many people do. And if it doesn't happen, after many years, we may dismiss it and say, "Maybe it wasn't really God's will," or, "He resisted."

But the stronger way to pray about the unsaved is to visualize them already Christian, to accept the fact that they will be saved, just as you accepted the fact that God touched you in Holy Baptism, or just as you accepted the fact that you were saved when you had a conversion experience. You accept the fact that God will answer your prayers. You believe even against the evidence, without sight, that the Lord will save the person. And the way to believe that is to visualize the person in church, to visualize them sitting meditating and thinking about the Lord, to visualize them singing out of a hymnbook in Sunday morning worship, to visualize them leading devotions with the family at the table, on their knees with the children by the bed praying for them, writing out a tithe for the church offering envelope on Sunday, and to thank the Lord that he is delighted to hear your prayer. When something is as certain to be God's will as this is, then you can visualize it already being done, and it shall be so. That may be why Jesus thanked his Father before he raised Lazarus from the dead: by faith he had already seen it happen, and so he could just thank God.

In the same way one can visualize human relationships being healed. We know that it is not God's will that a marriage break up. I oftentimes visualize Jesus knocking on the door of a home where there is a problem in the marriage, and in my imagination I see the husband or wife going to the door and inviting Jesus in. I see them discussing their problem with Jesus, and I see him telling them what's wrong. It's simply the word of God that he speaks, one that we already have in Scripture, like "Confess your faults to one another, and be healed," or "Parents, don't provoke your children to anger, but bring them up in the fear and admonition of the Lord," or "Honor your father and mother that it may be well with you, that your days may be long upon the land that the Lord your God gives you." And I see Jesus with his arms around both the husband and wife; I see the healing light come from him, like the halo we see around his head, except that the healing light comes from his whole body, enveloping both husband and wife. I see the walls between them coming down. I refer to all of this in the prayer, maybe with my hands upon both of them. Or if both are at a distance, I visualize Jesus actually healing the marriage relationship. The same is true with relationships between parents and children: I see Jesus healing the relationship by holding the child and holding the parents, and bringing them all together.

Our Financial Needs

Like any father, God wants to care for all our needs. He wants us to trust him and be dependent on him for our living. It is not God's will that anyone be poor or hungry. We can allow him to care for us in our times of need, as we can be his instruments to help others in our times of plenty. During the past year we have learned at the Life Institute that what we knew about for many years but hadn't actively believed, in the sense of testing it, is true: that God owns all the wealth in the world. The earth is the Lord's, and all its fullness. He will support that which he has willed into being. We have also learned that we do not need to go to specific individuals who have money and "work on" them in order that they can be used to provide money for us. What we do is visualize the Lord touching the hearts of people around the country who can bless and be blessed by giving. We have discovered that the Lord desires us to give, not just because work needs supporting, but because he wants to bless us with more; for the more we give, the more we will receive.

Many times we have learned that if we just trust him, God will come through. Sometimes we have wondered if he knew what he was doing. We have lived from day to day, provided with manna in the wilderness. We have not known the day before payday where in the world our paychecks were going to come from. We have truly learned the meaning of "daily bread," and have learned that it is sufficient. In our prayers we visualize the envelopes of money going into our mailbox. We have visualized all the bills being paid. And in the course of time every single bill has been paid, even during the six months I was laid up with a heart attack and heart surgery and could not conduct missions. It had to be God who did it, for there is no way that we could support the building and staff we have in the Life Institute were it not for God touching the people of his church. Funds come sometimes from people we don't even know, but who desire to help.

I think that the same discoveries may apply to your personal finances: pray with visualization that your needs will be met. Don't expect more than your "daily bread," sufficient for each day. Thank the Lord that he does supply your needs. Bless others, as you have been blessed.

Praying for Lost Things

I think that we can say that God specializes in lost things, and I have learned that it is all right to pray for God's help in finding that which has been lost. Psychiatrists tell us that when we misplace something, our deep mind may well tell us where we lost it. God speaks to our deep mind, and prayer can help us to recall where the misplaced item is.

God can help us retrieve the irretrievable as well. A good example of this is an experience I had with a ring which was given to me by a confirmation class in the late 1960s. The ring is beautiful: it is gold, and has a fish symbol on it, with a little cross where the eye of the fish would be. Some years ago I was swimming in Loon Lake, in eastern Washington state. I was out from the docks a distance and had been in the water for some time, when the ring fell from my finger into the lake. It went to the bottom in water ten feet deep. My family and I went diving for it, and succeeded only in stirring up the muck at the bottom of the lake. After two days of searching, we were ready to give up. I went upstairs to the cabin where we were vacationing, and got down on my knees and asked the Lord to find the ring. I said, "If you caused the ax-head to float in the Old Testament, you can make a ring float to the surface of a lake." And I visualized that ring floating to the surface, and I visualized myself standing on the dock and seeing the sun shine on it. After praying, I thanked the Lord that it would be so, and I went out and started watching for that ring to come up.

My family didn't know what I was doing, because I was hiding the fact that I was watching for it. But I really believed that God was going to cause that ring to float. As I was standing there watching, two or three days after the ring had been lost, a man wearing tanks on his back and flippers came down the back steps from the cabin. He had been called by a relative of ours from the power company. He was the man who dived underwater to help when dams were built. He asked, "Is this the place where the ring was lost? I'm here to look for it."

He went down, and after 20 minutes of pouring dirt on the bottom of the lake through a screen he came up with the ring and asked, "Is this it?" We have home movies of this find, showing all of us jumping up and down and hugging one another and the diver. One thing I learned from this is that, whenever possible, God uses the normal processes of nature for answering prayer. He set up the laws of nature for a purpose, and he doesn't go around breaking them. In this case he used a diver. He heard my prayers through the relative who called the diver and through the diver who did the searching. I still have that ring, to remember that answer to prayer.

Prayer for Animals

One of the things that Agnes Sanford taught me is that it is possible to pray for animals. When I told one of my friends about praying for animals, he was suspicious of the whole thing. I even forgot that I had mentioned it to him until he told me sometime later that he had taken his dog to the vet a number of times for eye problems that didn't respond to medication. He finally took the dog out behind the garage, hoping that his wife wouldn't see him, got down on his knees and put his hands on the dog's head, and said, "I'm a creature of God, and you're a creature of God. I'm created in the image of God, and you aren't. You are created for our enjoyment, but the Father watches over you just as he watches over every sparrow. So now I'm going to ask his light and his life to enter into your body, that your own immune system will fight off this illness, and that you will be perfectly healed." He thanked the Lord that he heard his prayer and that it was going to be so. He must have felt foolish down on his hands and knees praying for a dog; but God honors that kind of humility and faithfulness.

I have taught veterinarians around the country about praying for animals. I will never forget a veterinarian taking me out for lunch, and saying, "I want to report to you about what's happened." He had been praying for animals for over a year. He said that at his large clinic he did all the general surgery and had done 1018 surgeries in the past year, losing only four animals. He reported this to a group of veterinarians, who asked what his methods were, and kidded him about his having some method of surgery that they didn't know anything about. He was embarrassed, but he said, "Do you guys really want to know what it is?" And in front of the whole group of veterinarians, he said, "I pray for every animal I perform surgery on." As one might expect, they all groaned. But my friend knows that the unusual success he has in surgery is because he prays for animals. Since they are creatures of the earth as we are, and since God gives them life, the healing light of God's presence can also enter into them and heal their bodies.

Praying for Protection

One of the many things we can pray for with visualization is protection. I wonder how many churches realize that they could pray for the power of the Lord to protect their churches. Instead of installing sophisticated alarm systems, they could see holy angels encircling their church so that no thief would be able to break in and steal. I don't know of a church where regular prayers are prayed for the building and what's in it that anything ever gets touched. That's why some churches can leave their doors open and nothing happens, while other churches need to be locked and have fences around them. I believe there are protecting angels who are more than happy to protect the Lord's house.

Travelers can always benefit from prayer for a safe trip. We'll never know how many plane and car accidents have been avoided through prayer. When a member of my family is traveling, we pray for their protection, often visualizing angels around the car or supporting the wings of the plane, keeping everything running smoothly and keeping away danger. There are many instances where prayers for protection or assistance are in order, in all areas of life.

Perhaps more prayers for protection and prevention should be prayed. One of the striking things about the requests we receive to pray for people is that so many of the situations are desperate: we hear from people after the doctor has given them up, after the marriage is broken, after the accident occurs. It would be better if we prayed and were prayed for more regularly throughout our lives, in the calm, safe times as in the desperate. God is the source of everyday health and safety, as well as of saving acts and dramatic healings.

8

THE MYSTERY OF SUFFERING

In his second letter to the Corinthians Paul gives a bit of autobiography that is tantalizing in its brevity. He says, "And to keep me from being too elated by the abundance of revelations, a thorn was given me in the flesh, a messenger of Satan, to harass me" (2 Cor. 12:7 RSV). Many commentators have linked this passage to other statements in Paul's letters which hint at a bodily infirmity. In Galatians 4:13 he says, "As you know, it was bodily illness that originally led to my bringing you the gospel." Various writers have speculated that this "thorn in the flesh" was headache, temptation to lust, epilepsy, or eye problems. Paul never really says what it was, keeping the personal details in the background of his message. He does say that three times he asked the Lord for his problem to be removed, but it was not.

As praying Christians, we will have to face problems like Paul's many times, in people we may pray for and even in our own lives. What are we to think when suffering comes to us? And what should we think when, despite our sincere prayers, we and others do not become well? Suffering is actually harder for the Christian to understand than for the nonbeliever. Suffering is just a fact for nonbelievers, but Christians know that God is all-powerful, and could prevent it. It is hard to reconcile the existence of an all-loving and good God with the existence of suffering in the world. The problem of suffering is as old as history, and we shall not know the answers to it until we see God. But, on the basis of Scripture and experience, we can compare the merits of some of the theories about suffering.

Causes of Suffering

Many people label everything that happens on the stage of the world as God's will, including suffering. But we must first of all remember that God gave us free will, and he never violates that free will. While his grace is everywhere, the laws of nature, which God created, seem to forbid his grace entering into a situation unless it is asked to. Thus many things happen simply through the malice, stupidity, hatred, or carelessness of people, or through the chance occurrences of nature. An automobile accident, for example, cannot be said to have been God's will, especially if the accident involved a drunk driver, human error, or mechanical failure. If God entered our lives and prevented all errors, without our asking, we would not be free to make our own mistakes and to live with their consequences; we would not have free will. Time and chance happen to all people. Accidents, disease, and suffering, health and healing, like the rain and the sun, come to the just and the unjust alike.

There are many things, then, in the daily events of life which cannot be said to have happened for any particular reason. Trying to pinpoint reasons and meanings for a suffering person is liable only to add insult to injury. It is far too easy to see unfortunate occurrences as punishment or warning. Jesus said of the blind man, "It is not that this man or his parents sinned;

he was born blind so that God's power might be displayed in curing him" (John 9:3). He also said of some people of his time who had met with disaster, "Do you imagine that, because these Galileans suffered this fate, they must have been greater sinners than anyone else in Galilee? I tell you they were not" (Luke 13:2-3). The Hebrews thought, as did Job's accusers, that God was the author of suffering as well as the healer of our diseases. Many people today still believe this. Jesus showed that this is not the case.

Even if we don't know the reasons for suffering, there are many causes. Some suffering is the result of the operation of the inexorable laws of nature. You don't break the law of gravity, you demonstrate it. The laws of nature are given to make life orderly; without law life would be chaos. Some suffering comes because of the fact that as humans we are all members of one another. We are mixed together and in relationship, and that can produce conflict.

Hell can be pictured as a place where everyone is seated at tables laden with sumptuous food, but cannot eat because their arms are bound so that they cannot bend them, and so they go hungry. Heaven, then, can be pictured as a place where there are the same tables, and where the people have the same bound arms, but where everyone is happy—because they feed each other. Relationships are double-edged; they can both hurt and help.

We often hear people say, "God caused that to happen to teach me patience." James, of course, says, "My brothers, whenever you have to face trials of many kinds, count yourselves supremely happy, in the knowledge that such testing of your faith breeds fortitude, and if you give fortitude full play you will go on to complete a balanced character that will fall short in nothing" (James 1:2-4). But a little further on he says, "No one under trial or temptation should say, 'I am being tempted by God'; for God is untouched by evil, and does not himself tempt anyone" (James 1:13-14). God does not send misfortunes to us. Life brings with it enough trials and sorrows; there will always be times when we are caught off guard and must go through trials. As carefully as we protect ourselves, suffering is bound to cross our path. But we must not attribute that suffering to God. Even Paul makes clear that his "thorn" was "Satan's messenger"—not God's.

The Question of Unanswered Prayer

A difficult question for Christians is why our prayers for healing and assistance sometimes are apparently not granted, as Paul's requests were not. I don't think we will ever know the complete answer to this. It will remain a mystery, just as it is a mystery why some people are not saved.

It is my experience that sometimes the problem lies with the prayer itself. Perhaps the illness which we seek to have healed is a symptom of something else which should be resolved, but which hasn't been discovered or prayed for yet. I have found that migraine headaches, for example, will not respond to prayer unless the reason for them has been removed. The disease will not go away until what it has to say has been heard. Sometimes the faith of the pray-er is not strong enough, as Jesus often pointed out to his disciples. Sometimes the will to live is not strong enough, and the body cannot be called into action to help itself. Many people just don't want to accept the responsibilities of wholeness. Sometimes unforgiveness stands in the way. Sometimes an illness is beyond the body's restorative abilities, when tissue damage is too extensive or when a limb has been lost.

But there are always the cases where the conditions seem good, but the request is not granted. In these cases, as in all suffering, we must recognize that, while God does not send suffering, and though suffering may indeed be "Satan's messenger," sometimes God does *allow* suffering to remain. This, of course, does not mean that we should seek suffering, or that we should not seek its removal. Paul prayed three times for his affliction to be removed, and even Jesus prayed to be relieved at Gethsemane.

I often hear people talking about "redemptive suffering" and "completing the sufferings of Christ." If we accept all the suffering which comes our way, we will have much needless misery. I think that only ten percent of our pain is what could be called redemptive suffering. Most pain makes us turn inward upon ourselves much more than if we didn't have it. If you have ever seen mentally ill people, you know that they are not being redeemed by their suffering, and neither is anyone else.

"Completing the sufferings of Christ," as the New Testament speaks of it, is, I believe, suffering for the sake of the gospel. Being ill usually does nothing earthshaking for the gospel. Suffering rejection, grieving for other people, sharing their burdens, even being imprisoned like Paul—all these go along with the task of spreading the gospel. But there is no reason for us to suffer illness or sorrow when we don't have to.

The Value of Suffering

For some reason, however, God allows the "thorn" to remain in that ten percent of cases. Somehow in the seeds of suffering there is life and wholeness. In these cases it may seem that our prayers are not being answered; but in fact they are being answered differently than we had expected. The answer to Paul's prayer was not, "Be made well," but, "My grace is all you need." Paul's ministry was not harmed by his affliction, but helped; the same affliction might have caused a different person to retreat into a shell. Each of us is unique, and God does not treat us all alike. He does not ask more than we can give; he does not put us through more than we can bear. Suffering is, in this sense, tailor-made. If our prayers for healing or help are not answered, we must ask, "What can I learn from this?" Often the answer leads to a healing of the spirit, even if the body is not healed. God is concerned with our wholeness, not just the relief of symptoms. God will give us better things than we can even ask for.

There is a tremendous power in suffering to chisel the spirit and beautify the character. We sometimes see the finest qualities in life because of trouble. If there were no danger, there would be no chivalry or fortitude. If there were no suffering, there would be no compassion. If there were no discipline or hardship, there would be no patient endurance. If there were no temptation, what would it mean to be righteous? The greatest light into the meaning of suffering for a Christian is that it trains us for our high calling as children of God. God is interested in our eternal life, and he is working to prepare us for it. Most of the noise about suffering comes from the spectators, not the sufferers. James 1:2-4 is an important passage to remember. If you could turn your life back 10, 20, or 30 years, would you eliminate the sorrow and hardship? Underneath all suffering, said Søren Kierkegaard, is the sacrament of God's love.

We are reduced, finally, to raw trust in God's mercy and wisdom, faith in God's love even in the face of overwhelming difficulty. As I write this, that is where I find myself. After three heart attacks (two on the operating table) and two open-heart surgeries, I not only have walked through the valley of death and depression, but I am learning to live without any answer to my "Why, Lord?" Perhaps I will learn the answer someday. But right now, the Answerer is enough.

9

THE GIFT OF PRAYER

In Luke 17 we read that Jesus met ten lepers on his way to Jerusalem. In response to their pleas for help, he healed them. "One of them, finding himself cured, turned back praising God aloud. He threw himself down at Jesus' feet and thanked him." Then Jesus said, " 'Were not all ten cleansed? The other nine, where are they? Could none be found to come back and give praise to God except this foreigner?' " (vv. 15-18).

We often see people like these ten lepers in our ministry. It seems as though one of the chief effects of suffering, especially mental suffering, is that it draws sufferers in on themselves. They are concerned primarily with themselves and their illness. This self-centeredness often makes things difficult for the pray-er, although we know that we are commanded to love especially the unlovable. But unfortunately, this self-centeredness can also stand in the way of their healing. Ingratitude can be as big a block as unforgiveness. To the one leper who returned to give thanks, Jesus said, " 'Your faith has cured you' "

(Luke 17:19). We can suppose that, while the nine received relief from their disease, this man alone received salvation.

Prayer is the place to thank God, to praise him, to come to know him. We can become so caught up in the excitement of prayers of petition, and answers to prayer, that we neglect prayers of worship and of contemplation. While prayer for others is certainly unselfish, we must not forget our own prayer relationship with God. We should not spend all our prayer time asking things of God, even on someone else's behalf. That is why it is important to begin and end prayers for healing with praise and thanksgiving, and why we must take time to refresh ourselves in meditative prayer. It is not good to partake of only one kind of prayer, just as it is not good to eat only one food. "Give, and gifts will be given you" (Luke 6:38). Prayer is God's gift to us; but it can also be our gift to him. In prayer we can give of ourselves to God.

Some people find that they can get only so far in the process of their own healing, and then they come to a standstill. Perhaps this happened to the other nine lepers. The problem may be that as they have "frozen" their gratitude, taking without giving, so they have frozen their healing. It seems as though in giving you create a vacuum in yourself. Nature abhors a vacuum, and so by giving you are at once filled up again. Giving—whether by sharing the gift of prayer, by giving financially to God's work, or by giving God the gift of your praise and worship—is a key to healing and wholeness. In prayers of petition we come to *depend on* God; but it is in prayers of praise and listening that we come to *know* God.

Praise and Thanksgiving

Praise is the natural response of the creation to its Creator. Praise takes time: time to contemplate the wonders of God and creation, time to offer our appreciation. We seem to have lost our sense of wonder today. This has been a century of brilliant achievement and amazing discoveries; yet in the last quarter of a century the popular theme has not been so much "brave new world" as "the wasteland." We barely bat an eye at human journeys into outer space or the world of the atom. Everyday life is so routine that many turn toward drugs and eastern philosophies as a way to escape or to "heighten" consciousness. The fast pace of our lives today has caused us to overlook the wonder of everyday things and the importance of being connected with that for which our heart yearns, our Creator, our Lord and our God.

The psalmist says, "Take the veil from my eyes, that I may see the marvels that spring from thy law" (Ps. 119:18). One of the prayers I pray regularly is, "Open my eyes, Lord, to see things as they really are." In time he is causing some of the scales to fall from my eyes. God is like the sun: we may not look directly on his face, but we see his glory reflected in his creation, as in the burning bush, while we watch the world come to life under his loving and creative touch. I have found that a good way to retrieve a sense of wonder is to read books on science written for the lay person. Books on astronomy, physics, and medicine are full of fascinating facts. For some reason these facts seem to stick easily in my mind.

For example, as a passenger on the earth you are racing around the sun at 70,000 miles per hour. Our solar system is orbiting in its galaxy faster than 500,000 miles per hour. Yet we are unaware of it; our senses fail us here. Imagine the sun as being shrunk to the size of a six-inch ball. The earth would then be the size of a bead about one-sixteenth of an inch in diameter, revolving around the sun at a distance of less than 20 paces. The moon would resemble a tiny grain of pepper two or three inches from the earth. Mars would be like a grain of salt ten paces beyond the earth. Jupiter would be a marble 100 paces from the sun; Saturn, a bit smaller than Jupiter, would be 70 paces beyond Jupiter. Pluto, the last planet in our solar system, would be another grain of salt some 4/10 of a mile from the sun. Such would be the dimensions of our solar system, reduced 9 billion times. And this solar system is an almost insignificant part of a galaxy containing more than 100 billion stars, many of them far larger than our sun, a galaxy so huge that a light ray traveling more than 11 million miles per minute would take roughly 100,000 years to travel it from end to end. And the galaxy is only a speck in the great universe. Yet in all the hugeness of space, even the hairs on your head are numbered by God.

One drop of water contains one billion billion atoms (that's 1 with 18 zeroes after it). Each atom is mostly empty space. If the nucleus of an atom were enlarged to the size of a golf ball, its electrons could be likened to flies flying around the golf ball half a mile away. The distance between atoms this size would amount to thousands of miles. If all the space between and inside each atom in the Washington Monument were removed, the resulting compressed matter would be smaller than a sewing needle. Yet because of the intense energy in the atom, and the speed of the orbits of its components, matter appears solid. Your body contains 10 billion-billion-billion atoms (1 with 28 zeroes after it). And the Creator of all of this dwells within you, and calls you his child. Read Psalm 8 to find an expression of awe at this.

As the psalmist says, "The heavens tell out the glory of God, the vault of heaven reveals his handiwork" (Ps. 19:1). When you have contemplated the works of God, and find that you are speechless, read the Psalms, and let their timeless words speak for you. Psalms 148 and 150 are particularly suited to the prayer of praise, as are many others. There is no special time or place to praise God. Praise is always appropriate, and always life-giving and healing. Praise lifts us out of ourselves, and places us in the presence of the Father.

I think that one of the greatest prayers ever uttered by a human being, outside of Jesus himself, was spoken by the man who cried out to Jesus on behalf of his son, "I believe; help my unbelief!" (Mark 9:24 RSV). We could rephrase this prayer for our purposes here, "We give thanks; help our unthankfulness." Most of us remember to thank God for the good things that come to us. But we forget to thank God for everything that happens to us, including everyday events and misfortune and setbacks. Paul said, "Be always joyful; pray continually; give thanks whatever happens; for this is what God in Christ wills for you" (1 Thess. 5:16-18).

Ingratitude must grieve God's heart. As Shakespeare's King Lear said, "How sharper than a serpent's tooth it is to have a thankless child." If we are hurt when our children forget to thank us for a gift, how it must wound God's great heart when we fail to show gratitude to him, who gave us the gift of life itself.

Too often we ask, "What have you done for me today, Lord?" forgetting that each day is a gift from God. "This is the day which the Lord has made; let us rejoice and be glad in it" (Ps. 118:24 RSV). Jesus said, "The man who can be trusted in little things can be trusted also in great" (Luke 16:10). I think we can say also that the one who is grateful for a little will have much to be grateful for. In our ministry we have learned to be as grateful for the widows' mites as for the large gifts that come out of abundance.

It is not enough just to say, "Thank you for my blessings." We need to take a little time to enumerate and meditate on our blessings. And we must thank God for our misfortunes, too. Read the first chapter of James again. We know that while God does not send trouble to us, he does bring good out of it. In thanking God we prepare ourselves to await and seek out the good which God will bring. We thank God whether we feel like it or not, for there is no better way to *feel* grateful than to *act* grateful.

I would like to share with you a prayer of thanksgiving I wrote while I was recovering from my second heart attack:

Dear God,

I love you and apologize for not showing it more. I'm helpless to do anything unless you enable me. Teach me how to pray.

Thanks for creating this world with its billions of planets and billions of light-years of space.

Thanks for the planet Earth and all that is on it and in it.

Thanks for people, the animals, the birds, the fish, the insects, the trees, the bushes, the flowers, and the rocks. Thanks for the sand and the mighty oceans, the clouds, the sun, and all the beautiful stars.

Thanks for the prophets, for Abraham, Isaac, Jacob, Joseph, Moses, and for Israel as a nation.

Thanks for Jesus of Nazareth. I've never seen him, but I love him dearly. He's done so much for me. Thanks, Jesus, for breaking down the door of the prison house I was in and throwing open the door to the Father's house. Thank you, Jesus, for your life, death, and resurrection. Thank you, Jesus, that you know me and that you have "redeemed me, a lost and condemned creature."

Thanks, Father and Son, for your blessed Holy Spirit, who calls, gathers, enlightens, and sanctifies the whole Christian church on earth. Thanks for calling me and sanctifying me. Thanks for empowering me for witness and blessing me with fruits and gifts.

Thanks for the hope of eternal life. Thanks for the opening chapters here and now, but thanks most of all that our names are written in heaven.

Thanks for Christian parents who took me to church when I was three days old and gave me to the Lord. Thanks for my baptism at one month of age, which made me your child. Thanks that no matter how far I strayed from that, you never left me. Thanks for never letting me go.

Thanks for a beautiful and loving wife who has stood with me for all these years. Thanks for her encouragement and love and trust, for her bearing six amazing children as the fruit of our love. Take care of them all, Lord, and please never let go of them, either.

Thanks for the pain in life as well as the joys. Thanks for death, which is the ultimate birth.

I am so grateful that you are in charge. I'm looking forward to being in your presence and enjoying you forever.

In Jesus' name, Amen.

Christian Meditation

When we consider God's works and ways in preparation for praise and thanksgiving, we are actually engaging in meditation. Many Christians are suspicious of meditation, even Christian meditation, because they have been warned about Transcendental Meditation and other non-Christian mystical and eastern disciplines. It is helpful to remember that an important difference between Christianity and other religions is that while most religion is the human search for God, Christianity is God's search for human beings. Christianity is not a quest for enlightenment. We believe because we are called to believe, we can believe only if God enables us to. That is why I stress the point that prayer is *response* to God. In Christian meditation we do not primarily seek a mystical experience or union with God which does away with our own identity. We try to be receptive to God's presence, to open our inner ears to hear what he has to say.

Christian meditation centers around Christ and is based on his redemptive work. In meditation I picture Christ in almost all the "imaging" scenes. I also make the sign of the cross to symbolize the heart of the message. Martin Luther urged us to make the sign of the cross each day, as a remembrance of our baptism. Making the sign of the cross, repeating the names "Jesus" or "Father," praying certain prayers or singing certain songs, are not magical tricks for getting into God's presence, but only ways to prepare the mind and heart to receive his presence. Meditation may be nothing more than sitting quietly and listening or thinking about God; or it may involve the imagination, putting yourself in the midst of a Bible story or other scene. A "side effect" of meditation, by the way, is that it reduces stress.

Besides being the subject of many Christian classics, there is biblical precedent for meditation. The psalmist says, "Let the words of my mouth and the meditation of my heart/be acceptable in thy sight, O Lord, my rock and my redeemer" (Ps. 19:14 RSV); " 'Be still, and know that I am God' " (Ps. 46:10 RSV); "Wait quietly for the Lord, be patient till he comes" (Ps. 37:7); "My mouth shall speak wisdom; the meditation of my heart shall be understanding" (Ps. 49:3 RSV): "Truly my heart waits silently for God" (Ps. 62:1); "I meditate upon all thy works and muse on all that thou hast done" (Ps. 77:12). In these passages, the psalmist probably is using the word "meditation" to mean something like "deep thought"; and meditation is as simple as that. I believe that when Jesus went up on the mountain and out into the wilderness, he did so so he could meditate with a minimum of distraction. The wording of the Psalms makes clear that in meditation we listen to God with our heart, or spirit, and not as much with the conscious mind.

I like to use my imagination in meditation, picturing myself in a Bible story or a situation of my own invention. The mind is very susceptible to pictures and sensations. God can touch us powerfully through the imagination. You might imagine yourself as one of the blind men Jesus healed, for example. Imagine the sounds of a busy street of Jesus' time—the people talking excitedly, the donkeys braying. Smell the fresh-baked bread, the tired animals. Feel the dust stirred up by the people passing by. Feel the apprehension of a helpless blind man, not knowing what all the excitement is about, but hearing people calling out to the Son of David. Imagine the touch of Jesus' hands on your eyes, the feeling of warmth and trust stirring in your breast. See the shadowy figures that appear before your eyes as your healing begins. Feel the gratitude that springs from your heart.

Many Bible stories can be used in this way. If you use your God-given imagination to call forth every detail of the experience, you will find yourself touched just as surely as the person in the story. Meditation of this kind can be done in a group, with one person reading the story very slowly and making suggestions, while the others sit with their eyes closed. Or you might be able to use a tape recorder, so you don't have to distract yourself by reading, unless it is a story you know by heart.

You can also make up your own situation. Many people like to keep in their minds a special place—an imaginary garden, or park, or bridge by a stream, or cabin—where they can meet and be with Jesus. With some practice, you will find that you can talk to Jesus with your heart, and wait and listen for his answers. They will come.

When you first begin, it is difficult to keep up meditation for more than 15 minutes at a time without becoming distracted or tired; but you will find that with time and practice you become more accustomed to it. Don't be frustrated if you don't seem to be having any kind of special feeling during meditation. It may be that the only feeling or experience you have is one of relaxation. But your aim is not to have a special experience or vision. It is to place yourself in a position of receptivity to God, to offer your love and invite his presence. Soon you will find that he is leading you.

10

THE HUMAN SPIRIT

In western culture we have almost ceased to believe that human beings are made up of anything more than mind and body. Yet the most important, all-encompassing part of us is our spirit, the part that is most sensitive to our relation to God. It is through our spirit that we receive life, the Holy Spirit, creativity, communication with God, the gifts of the Spirit. It is the spirit that in these difficult times becomes wounded, imprisoned, ignored. It is a part of us that many people have never known.

I want to stress the importance of the human spirit in order to put into perspective the role of prayer, especially prayer for healing, prosperity, and other requests. For God is concerned for our welfare, just because he loves us; but, above all else, he is concerned about our spiritual welfare, our life in the resurrection. We have free will, to choose God or not, and God does not violate that freedom. But he will do all that is possible to woo or to hound us. To pray for physical healing or prosperity without looking out for our spiritual side is almost like "using" God—taking gifts from him without entering into a relationship with him.

God is the author of all healing, whether the instrument is medical science or prayer. God sends his healing to all his creatures, worthy or unworthy. God heals most of our diseases through the natural order. I don't think that Christians are any more likely to be healed than non-Christians, except by prayer uttered in faith. Sometimes non-Christians have less "clutter" and more real faith and openness than some so-called Christians. I have prayed for many non-Christians who were subsequently healed and who ultimately gave their hearts to Jesus.

The Spiritual Dimension

What makes illness and healing, or any kind of answer to prayer, different for the Christian is the spiritual dimension. The Christian who is aware of his or her spiritual nature receives an extra measure of healing. The Christian acknowledges the Healer, God, and can give thanks to him; thus the Christian is spared from the exaggerated self-consciousness of illness and lifted into God-consciousness. The Christian can also learn the meaning of illness. I have learned, for example, that my past heart problems have been saying to me not only "Take it easy," but also "Let life get to your heart. Open up the tunnel between your heart and your head." My heart condition, at least to some degree, has been a mirror of my spiritual condition. Just as my physical heart was starved for oxygen-rich blood, so my spiritual heart was starved for the love of God. I might have gotten well without prayer; but I doubt it, and I'm sure I would not have learned what I did.

God wants us to know what illness and misfortune and answers to prayer are saying to us. Body, mind, and spirit are so closely tied together that what affects one affects the others. The story of Adam and Eve mirrors the life of each human being. The unfallen Adam and Eve could listen to God and hear him. They had constant communion with the life-giver. They were God-conscious, and not self-conscious; they were incapable of duplicity and could show their whole selves to God. They were unified in body, mind, and spirit, and had authority over all nature, as well as over themselves. They were in accord with the perfect will of God. Their minds contained no bad memories, no poor self-image, no repressed desires, no feelings of rejection. They were filled with the Spirit of God. All their relationships were relationships of love. Their bodies suffered no illness.

When Adam and Eve fell, their entire lives changed. Self-will is the sin of the Fall. It is the basic sin behind all sins. We reenact the Fall every day. In rebellion against God's will, we become separated from God. We have all cut ourselves off from the source of life. The mind, separated from the will of God, falls prey to evil thoughts and pride. The body, separated from the source of life, falls ill. All disease and all disharmony are the result of the Fall.

Wholeness Restored

"Sin" means, among other things, "missing the mark." Illness, corruption, and unrest on earth are not so much punishment for sin as they are the consequences of separation from the Life-giver, just as a tree will die if it is uprooted from the earth. The human spirit still yearns for God, though. When touched by God's Holy Spirit, our spirit seeks to lead the mind, will, emotions, and body back to God. It seeks to unify human beings, who became fragmented in the Fall. True wholeness is to choose the heaven of the integrated and emancipated self rather than the hell of the disintegrated self in separation and bondage. Wholeness is to choose the same love that has bound together the Father and Son throughout eternity. It is to enter the great dance of healthy relationship with the self, with others, with God, with his creation.

Your spirit is the "real you." "Among men, who knows what a man is but the man's own spirit within him?" (1 Cor. 2:11). We need to learn to know our own spirit. Today we seem to think that our mind is the deepest part of us. It is not. The spirit—the little child of God inside you, if you are a Christian —is the deepest and truest part of you. Just as the Holy Spirit is the most elusive part of the Trinity, so our spirit is the most elusive or shyest part of us. But it may well be our point of contact with God.

The mind and body we now have will someday be recreated in spirit. St. Paul says, "All flesh is not the same flesh: there is flesh of men, flesh of beasts, of birds, and of fishes—all different. There are heavenly bodies and earthly bodies; and the splendor of the heavenly bodies is one thing, the splendor of the earthly, another" (1 Cor. 15:39-40). He continues, "Sown as an animal body, it is raised as a spiritual body. If there is such a thing as an animal body, there is also a spiritual body" (1 Cor. 15:44). Paul does not say that we will be *spirit,* but a *spiritual body.* We will no longer *have* a body; we will *be* one. We will at last be at perfect harmony and unity, within and without. All that is unique and good in us, in our body, mind, will, and emotions, will be recreated in spirit, will be drawn up into the life of Christ.

Our spirit holds the promise of the resurrection. I think I am beginning to know my spirit. Like so many of you, I have dwelt long on my sinfulness. I've thought of myself in the worst possible terms. There is a difference, however, between being a sinful human being and being a rotten pile of garbage. As seriously as I must take it, the sinful part of my personality is in the long run superficial. In fact, the root of the word *personality* is the Greek word *persona,* which meant a mask worn by an actor in a Greek drama. Since I am in Christ, the sinful me is not the "real me" at the core of my being. At the core of my being is the part of me that God looks at and that yearns for God. It is the part of me that is "without blemish and innocent in his sight" (Col. 1:22). In Christ, we are a "new creation." It is the inner part of me that is endowed, surrounded, indwelt, filled, and energized with the blessed Trinity. "You are not in the flesh, you are in the Spirit, if the Spirit of God really dwells in you" (Rom. 8:9 RSV). As long as I dwell excessively on the sinful part of myself, beyond healthy repentance and confession, I cannot come to understand or know that God really dwells in me. I must come to recognize that my spirit has been connected with God's Spirit. If we could only learn to see the spirit in one another, how much gentler and more loving we would be with one another! Inside the most wretched person is a little child of God yearning to be recognized.

The Spirit of God speaks to our own spirit; our spirit speaks to the unconscious mind; the unconscious mind influences the conscious mind and the body. The communication lines can work in reverse as well, as when our conscious prayers move our inner spirit. The "conscious" mind is not as conscious of God as our "unconscious" mind.

When I first started coming out of the anesthesia after my second open-heart surgery, I am told that my first words to my family were, "I am happy, and Jesus Christ is Lord." I was deeply touched when I heard later that I had said that. I can't take credit for it. I have no awareness or recollection of having said it. I know that it was my spirit, through my unconscious mind, speaking while my mind was asleep. The mind is willful, and wants to control people and circumstances. But the spirit is more in tune with the Spirit of Jesus; it is humble, childlike, meek, poor in spirit. It is the baby in us who was baptized. It is content to wait for God's touch. It is the part of us that is made in the "image of God."

Prayer is *response* to God. He takes the initiative; he directs the response. Our spirit hears his call. Our heart yearns for him. If we seek to release our spirit, and allow it free expression, it will be drawn toward God. Where the spirit leads, the rest of us follows. Through our spirit, the Spirit of God enters us and dwells in us, animates our every faculty and cell. The spirit finds its home and rest in God. Abundant life lies in the life of the Spirit, through Jesus Christ, who made it possible for us to have union with God again, through the cross. Our purpose in life, in the words of the Westminster Confession, is to "glorify God, and enjoy him forever." In the resurrection, we will enjoy him forever, in perfect harmony with him and the new creation. The only true wholeness lies in relationship with God—Father, Son, and Holy Spirit—in connectedness with the blessed source of all life.